Road Rage at Its Finest

by Gennaro Lombardi

DORRANCE
PUBLISHING CO
EST. 1920
PITTSBURGH, PENNSYLVANIA 15238

Dorrance Publishing Co
585 Alpha Drive
Suite 103
Pittsburgh, PA 15238
Visit our website at *www.dorrancebookstore.com*

ISBN: 978-1-4809-5512-7
eISBN: 978-1-4809-5489-2

Dedication

I would like to dedicate this book mainly to my father. To the man who is a real citizen of the road and tried to teach me to be the same way, even if it did not work. He works for the State of New Jersey Turnpike Highway Authority. He is a certified master diesel mechanic. He cares for the road, the vehicles that he fixes that travel up and down those roads, and most importantly, the people on the roads. He himself is a great driver and has not gotten a moving violation in over twenty-something years. Thanks, Dad, for helping fix all those cars and trucks that I broke time and time again. You are a good man.

I would also like to dedicate part of this book to all the Law Enforcement of America. To the men and women who risk their life and to go out on those crazy roads when we are speeding by and Road Raging. All they are doing is trying to keep us safe. If it was not for them, truly the roads would be like something out of a Mad Max film. We need the cops to stop us from Road Raging and killing one another.

And, I would also like to make a formal apology to everyone who I have ever cut off on the road in a fit of Road Raged. I am sorry, and I won't let it happen again, I hope!

Note from the Author

Hello, My Fellow Road Ragers,

My name is Gennaro Lombardi and I am an Italian American kid from Northern New Jersey. I grew up in one of the smallest towns in New Jersey, and I grew up in one of the smallest bodies, 5'5" height, 155 pounds for a man, but let me tell you that for certain that I had one of the biggest attitudes when it came to certain things, as most hothead hotheaded Italians with a size complex do.

I would say I, as I am sure most people that know me would say, is that I am one of the nicest people in the world 95 percent of the time, but the other 5 percent of the time I had a bit of an attitude when I felt like I was being belittled, so I would tend to lash out. As for instance, if you stood in front of me at a concert and you were taller than me and you blocked my view, I would have thrown whatever I had in my hands (pizza, soda, beer) right at the back of your head because I would I had to get back at your for belittling me. And that is if you did it on purpose or not. So if you are a tall person, next time you go to a concert make sure there is not a short Italian sitting behind you, because you don't want pizza to hit you in the back of your head.

And, of course, another one of those thing that would set me off and really expose my bad attitude and my little person complex was when I was behind the wheel of a car. If someone cut me off, God forbid, a fit of Road Rage was not a maybe, it was a mandatory. How dare you cut me off and try to belittle me!? I will show them!

Besides everything else in life that would set me off, though, Road Rage was truly at the top of the list, and it was something that I did for years and it was a big part of my life, actually.

And in fact, I would even sarcastically say that I started Road Raging before I ever even got into a car, and maybe, just maybe, I was born with it because of how young I was when these issues actually started.

Road Rage was a big part of my life, and even scarier thing to say is, is that I think I was even addicted to it for a while as there was not a day that I did not miss Road Raging for probably a couple of years. If I went out for a ride and someone did not bother me on the road, I would literally have to go out of my way to bother someone because if I did not get into at least one screaming or cursing contest with someone on the road at least once a day in my travels, I would not feel normal!

I would say Road Rage was even fun for many, especially when I was younger, as it was an amazingly fun thing to me to win a screaming competition in a fit of Road Rage with another person, it was a good time running cars into the ground, it was rush racing on the streets, and it was exciting destroying trucks when I would go off-roading in the woods, but as I got older and this behavior got worse and worse, change was bound to happen soon because it came to a point to where all this craziness kind of messed up my life. Though at the time, I never really thought that there was a problem, just as an alcoholic does not think that there is a problem with drinking a fifth of vodka before he walks into work, yet he goes in drunk and messes everything up and destroys the office, he does not know there is a problem until he loses his job, and the same went for me. I did not know there was a problem until I lost everything because of my Road Raging and crazy driving, and as a result of loss, I made me hit a low in my life that would inevitably lead me to a grand awaking in which I would be able to see my own faults.

There was many years of racing on the streets, Road Raging with people and getting into fights, getting pulled over, arguing with cops, getting ticket after ticket, getting my cars towed home or impounded, and just plain out beating on my cars until they were destroyed because I used to actually enjoy driving like an animal and beating the hell out of my cars.

All that crazy behavior lead to me to losing my driver's license for the grand number of four time by just the young age of twenty-four for having to many points. And if that isn't bad enough, even if I did have a valid driver's license, I had to walk to work (or ride my bike) anyway because at one time I had six broken-down cars in my yard and not one of them were even able to be driven because I had beaten them up so bad.

Yes, there is more. It even came to a point that when I did have a valid driver's license that was not suspended and I actually had a car that was able to be driven, not one of my friends or family would even get into to the car with me to drive anywhere anymore, not even to go to the hospital, because they all had enough of me and the way I drove.

So after going what I went through, and then hitting a low in my life, I finally came to a point to where I was forced to look back at my past and face it. In this vision of looking back at my past, I seen a man who was crazy, yes definitely, but I also seen a man who was smart. I saw a man that actually mastered the art of what Road Rage actually is.

And being that so, as the ancients believe, once you master something, then you can finally teach it teach it to those who wish to learn that which you now know so well.

So began that I now wanted to teach people about Road Rage, I began a quest a quest of studies so I could gather as much information from my past so I could use it to help others through real life experience.

I studied who I was in the past, what was I was going through mentally or emotionally that made me that way feel certain ways (such as anger or Rage), and was that truly making me do what I always did best, Road Rage.

In this small quest, the process of learning and growth (mentally and emotionally, not physically unfortunately as I am still short) I came up with a lot of answers to many of the questions that I had, and being that so I wrote down as much as I could as to keep a record, and to learn from that, and as to maybe use it blue print, or a Road Map if you will to help other not go down the same path that I did. Hence, this book.

I learned so much that in my journey that I now have my Road Rage under control, for the most part! Hey, even a master of karate has a bad day now and then I am sure and he ends up punching someone in the face who tries to walk into his house with his shoes on. It's all about respect, buddy, you know.

But I will have to say this, I truly believe that I have changed from being a good person 95 percent of the time to 99.99 percent (like Lysol) of the time, and that is big!

The process of change was not all easy, nor short, as it was kind of hard to go from the crazy kid that cut everyone off on the road day in and day out and literally loving to Road Rage, to then going onto to becoming a guy that drives around with a Buddha statue on his dashboard that he uses as a reminder to himself when he is driving alone as to slow the hell down. But I will have to use an old and corny saying here, and I will say that I believe that if I can do it, then I am sure you or anyone can do it, considering I was as bad as bad can get.

So in my miraculous change from the kid who holds the record in his home town that he grew up in for being pulled over more times than anyone else, to being the kid that learned how to wave at people instead of giving them the finger and throwing coffee at them, this is my story, and I would like to share it with you. But just be weary, as of course, I will be sharing the good and bad!

So read on my Road Raging friends and get ready to learn from the best of the best as to what Road Rage truly is all about.

Your Road-Raging Buddy,
Gennaro Lombardi

Chapter 1

What Is Road Rage? And Other Commonly Asked Questions!

What Is Road Rage?

Road Rage: Is aggressive or angry behavior by a driver of an automobile or other motor vehicle. Such behavior might include rude hand gestures (flipping the bird), verbal insults (yelling, "Up yours, buddy!"), deliberately driving in an unsafe manor (tailgating someone) or threatening manor (cutting someone off on purpose), and making verbal threats (yelling, "I am going kill you for cutting me off!").

Road Rage can lead to altercations (throwing you coffee at someone's car) on the road such as assaults (getting out of your car to kick someone's ass), and collisions (I did not mean to hit his car with my car, Officer) which can result in injuries (fake neck brace), and even death (not funny). It can be thought of as an extreme case of aggressive driving.

What Is an Aggressive Driver (or Road Rager)?

I do not like to refer to them as an aggressive driver, as I much rather like to refer to them as a Road Rager. Yes, I know Rager is not actually a word.

Road Rager: Is one of those people that we all know who is upset at the world, and they are usually they type of person that are very aggressive and angry by nature to begin with, so they lash out at the world because of their anger, and most commonly it comes out and shows up when they are behind the wheel of a car and it comes out in the angrily artistic form know as Road Rage, and hence, they become a Road Rager because they are the one doing the Road Raging.

A Road Rager is the person you see every day on your way to work and you witness them with their head of their car window and they are screaming out all of their life's frustrations on some other poor human that just stopped short in front of them by accident, as to let people walking cross the street, yet the Road Rager things that the person in front of them stopped short on purpose just to mess with them, so in response to the bad attitude and poor/wrong judgment, they will now have to verbally abuse the person that is in front of them for as long as it takes for him to feel justified.

Road Ragers are frequently connected to the people you know who have a Type-A personality. You know, the ones who are always in a rush and have no consideration for others, especially when on the road.

If the Road Rager is not behind the wheel of a car, you might recognize them and their Type-A personalities in your common everyday situations as so: People at home saying things to you like "The trash isn't going to take itself out, honey, so let's get to it!" People on the job that say such things as "Do you job quickly and there won't be a problem, A** H***!" And people who you come across when you are out in public and standing online at the grocery store and they end up behind you on line and you hear them huff and puff heavily, pretty much near hyperventilating, and then you turn around to see what the hell is going on, and as you look at them, they then look at their watch, look back up, give you, and then the cashier a wide-eyed aggressive look and then they blurt out as loud as they can, "What in the hell is taking so friggin' long!"

Road Ragers are the kind of people that are stressed out all day long and carry it around with them and spread it out on the rest of the poor world. The amount of stress that they carry is often so large and heavy that you will often see them driving a really big pickup up truck, as they need all that trunk space and the heavier shocks as to support all their baggage/problems.

Example Story: Picture it, you are a middle-aged (forty-year-old) white man who works in retail, and you are driving down the highway in your 2001 Subaru station wagon on your way home from work, and as you are in the right lane, you then start moving over and into the middle lane, and as you do, you then look in your rearview and see something odd, and as your focus come to a halt as to what is in your mirror, you see HIM!

There he is, the Road-Raging Rod Rager, who was driving down the road with his usual chip on his shoulder (really bad mood) as he his headed home from work also, and he is more upset than usual about his day at work, and he was just on his way home to go lash out at his family, but now you just tried to get in front of him as he is flying down the road and you slowed him down, God forbid.

So now and all of a sudden, as you are driving minding your own business, and not even realizing that you did anything wrong to this person you don't even know, this Road Rager is now behind you and they are beeping there horn at you like manic and then they trying to run you off the road with their car, literally. He wants to push you off of the road so you will crash.

You question in your head as to what the hell is going on, and is this person even real or not, and then when you look again, there he his, and now he is Road Raging even worse. Now the maniac is behind you and he is swerving back and forth like he is warming up his wheels like a NASCAR driver does just before a race, and he is tailgating you, he is beeping horn (and rather excessively), and now he even has his head out of his window and he is screaming and yelling profanity at you. Oh, wait, I forgot mention the best part. He is also making rude hand gestures (waving his middle finger in the air like they just don't care). And last but not least, the Road Rager is now in full on Road Raging mode and he is now starting to throw animate objects out of his car window (like his coffee or pocket change) and he is throwing them right at you.

When Road Rage gets to this stage, if you look closely enough in your rear view at the person doing the Road Rage behind you, but this is hard to do when you are trying to keep your eyes on the road, so don't try it, you will always notice that the Road Rager who is driving like a maniac, nine out of ten times they will have no seatbelt on, and they will only have one hand on their steering wheel, nonetheless. They are reckless and crazy in every sense.

There he is, the Road Rager, and now he is looking to take all his life's problems out on you, and why, all because you were trying to get over into their lane and you got a little too close to their car by accident. Man I feel sorry for you. You don't even know what you did wrong and there you are, getting chewed out (harassed) by this person you never even met before.

This story happens hundreds of times a day, all day, every day, and not only in America, but in every nation of that world that has more than one car on the road. So in revaluation of this, the only thing left to say is: As long as you have two cars driving on the road and one of those drivers has a bad attitude, Road Rage is possible.

What Makes Road Ragers So Out of Control?

Well, what is going on most of the time in a Road Rager's minds is this. They feel as if they are losing control of their lives in total essence, money, relationships, health, family, work, and once they feel as if they are losing control of these things in their life, they start to feel as if they are going to lose control of the main thing, their mind, where it is all stored.

Example Story: Picture it, you are a young, twenty-one-year-old female, African-American professional, and you are out walking your dog down the main road in town in which you live, and as you are walking and minding your own business, all of a sudden you hear some tires screech, and as you turn to look you see someone coming to an abrupt halt in their vehicle. You and your dog both get scared and look over as to see what happened simultaneously, and as you both do, you see a Road Rage altercation about to take place.

What you witness is that one guy cut another guy off on the road, you know, your usual Battle of the Bulge, and as their car came to a stop, the one the driver who was cut off now opens their car door right away and then they physically ejects themselves from their car at 100 miles per hour, and then the person runs over to the other driver vehicle who just cut him off. As this person takes off running, the second he gets over to the other persons car he them slams his hand down on the their vehicle, starts foaming from the mouth, and then he says to the other guy, "Move your car out of my way now A** H***, or I am going to kick your friggin' A**, man!" And as you witness this prehistoric event take place in front of you, you always say that one thing that we all say: "Look at that dude, HE HAS LOST HIS MIND!" and guess what, you are 100-percent right! Let me tell you what my Road Rage Buddha told me one time. The way you drive is truly a reflection of what is going on inside of you, on the outside. And from what I can see on the outside, I will then say this. Your inside is going way to fast, about ready to spin out of control, and crash.

More often than not, when people are Road Raging a lot in their lives, there is always way more going on in their lives in that moment then them just Road Raging. Something made them that way. There is always way more to the Road-Raging jerks story them him just being a Road-Raging jerk. Something or someone is making them crazy, and they are acting out.

How Bad Can Road Rage Get?

Road Rage comes in many formations also. It can be very mild-mannered (like Bruce Banner), such as a light beeping of the horn when you want to pass a car. Hey, you were just trying to be polite and let them know you are there and trying to pass. Then the car you beeped at politely flips you the bird for beeping at them and you both go your separate ways and that is it. Nothing more, nothing less. And in fact, we all wish that Road Rage was this light hearted all the time. You should always remember that one slogan: Easy come, easy go.

But Road Rage can also be very crazy and dangerous (LIKE THE HULK), and it can get to the point to where things can get very out of control very quickly, and if no one stops the situation early it can escalate into a very bad situation with people pulling over and fighting physically and hurting one another.

Example Story: Picture it, you are young twenty-four-year-old white, blue-collar male who is driving to work one morning in your 2002 Chevy Tahoe, when all of a sudden someone cuts you off.

Oh, wait, don't forget, as you were driving to work you were already in a bad mood to begin with, hey, you just woke up that way and you are a moody B**** sometimes, what can you do?

And now and even though you were just cut off, and you are in a bad mood, you would usually let something like that go, but that is not the case this time!

As the problem is, is that while you were driving, at the very moment you were cut off, you were also taking a sip off your coffee, and now, because the person cut you off and you were forced to jam on your breaks, you ended up moving forward to quickly, and the process, you ended up spilling your coffee all over you, your shirt, your pants, and your dashboard.

Your coffee has become a greater part of your outfit and your car then your cup. I know, don't things like this just seem to happen when you are already in a bad mood!?

Now come on. Are you the type of person who looks at the cup half full or half empty? If you said half full then you will think of it like this: "This is great, I have a new tie-dyed French vanilla coffee shirt on for work!" and then you just drive the opposite way.

If you are one who looks at the cup half empty type, this is how you will react. In your mind the person who cut you off needs to be punished severely because you just painting the inside of your car with coffee, you will either want vengeance, or at least a reimbursement for your coffee.

Now you say to yourself, "How dare that F****** A** H*** cut me off and make me spill my coffee!" And right after that, you then speed up and then go and cut the person off in return even worse.

Right after you do that, the situation then gets worse and worse and it escalates into you and this other person now swerving your cars in and out of traffic as to battle for first place, and almost causing a major accident on the road. And if that isn't bad enough, now the two for you start yelling at each other to pull over and fight, so you do. Hey, you aren't no chicken, right?

Now, you and this other Road Raging idiot both pull over and get out of your vehicles and approach each other. You both start yelling and then end up trying to kill one another physically! How did the Road Raging escapade turn out, you ask!? Who won, you ask!?

Let's put it this way, your opponent, yes, the person you just Road Raged at, just kicked the ever-loving S*** out of you, and bad! And guess what, after they knocked your ass down on the ground, they then ran away and they jumped back into his car and took off, and as they passed you they yelled really horrible profanities at you.

Yup, they left you all right there all F***** up on the side of the road, and if that isn't bad enough, now other people are driving by and they are laughing at you because the seen the whole incident. The instigator just got his ass kicked. Happens often, actually. "How is your day going so far?!" you ask. Your new tie-dyed French vanilla suit is now all torn apart to pieces, you got a fat bloody lip, one of your teeth just fell out of your mouth and into your hand, and you can barely get up because he also kicked you in the groin area. Bet you wish you had not stopped taking those Karate classes back in 1989, huh, pal? You got to be careful who you mess with.

Now call the boss and explain this one. This is you sobbing on the phone: "Hey, boss, I am sorry but I won't be making it in to work today. I just got beat up by Chuck Norris, literally, and I have to take myself to the hospital!"

Hopefully your boss is a funny guy like me and will understand, and he will just ask you if you got Chuck's autograph, and if you did, bring it into work tomorrow as redemption for not having a doctor's note for your callout.

So if you want to know, Road Rage can be anything from someone beeping their horn improperly to plain out having a physical altercation on the side of the road and trying to kill one another. It is no joking matter. You also have to remember one thing that my Road Rage Buddha told me: Road Rage is as bad as YOU make it!

Why Do Road Ragers Always Beep the Damn Horn?
To the normal people of the world it is known as the car horn. It is a very useful mechanism that is installed in automobiles and made to alert other people on the road so that they know that you are there. It can help you avoid accidents when someone is driving stupid. It can be used as a signal for help when in a dangerous situation, your boyfriend is on the hood of your car trying to punch the window through. Or it can be used to wake

that A** H*** sleeping at a green light in front of you and not moving. There are many advantages to having a horn, and it is actually mandated that all cars, or any vehicle that are street legal to have one installed on them.

But to people that Road Rage, the car horn is known as something very different. It is a whole different animal as they say. To people that Road Rage it is known as "the blow-off valve"!

The only way to explain it is like this. It's kind of like the boiler in your basement. Boilers have been known to build up too much pressure and explode, so what they have installed on them is a safety mechanism to relieve pressures called "the blow-off valve"! It stops it from exploding and releases all the pressure that the boiler cannot handle.

Road Ragers are the boiler, and the horn is the blow-off valve. The concept is identical. People that are Road Raging are under way too much pressure and usually fell like they are ready to blowup and they need to let it out quickly before they pop. So what do they do, they hold that horn down like a great big warning signal. *BEEEEEEEEEEP!*

That is why Road Ragers always beep the horn. They are warning you that they are hot and about ready to pop so you better look out. And much like the situation with a real boiler you have to be careful as to not go near it to because it could hurt and burn you. You have to wait for it to cool down first before going near it.

So best bet, when you hear someone treating their car horn like a factory whistle and you see steam coming out of that baby from them holding it down for so long, take it as a warning sign, someone is about ready to pop, and move the hell out of the way.

Why Do You Call Them Road Ragers And Not Aggressive Drivers?

I call them Road Ragers and not aggressive drivers because I have a theory. My theory kind of works like this.

A Road Rager can also be referred to as many things. Such as, an aggressive driver, a careless driver, and reckless driver, a lunatic on the road, an angry driver, or just plain out a maniac behind the wheel of a car!

Whatever you want to call them is fine. Road Rage, or what I like to refer to as the people who are actually doing the Road Raging are called Road Ragers, not an aggressive driver or any of the other words at this point.

An aggressive driver does drive aggressively, yes, but this book, is more about the person at their max point of anger, and that is when they are so mad that they actually past the point of aggressive driving and get enraged and lash out and start to really Road Rage at other drivers and people on the road. So therefore, they are past the point of being an aggressive driver and they are a Road Rager.

So because of my theory you will not see me refer to this word aggressive driver or aggressive driving that much in this book. It is such a political word to me also, and if there is one thing I am not, it's political.

And you know, I even tried to find out when this word aggressive driver that I do not like so much, was actually invented/spoken, but I could not find anything.

So in response to having an unanswered question, I had to at least a come up with a good example story/scenario in which it was created so at least we can have some fun.

Example Story: Picture it, it is the late 1950s, and there he was. A really big, white, old man who had no personality, no care for others, and loved nothing but money, and he was a powerful politician. Go figure, right?

"And where was he!" you ask. Where else besides being sitting in the back of his really big limousine and he is chauffeured around?

"And where was he going?" you ask. Where else besides back to his office after eating a really big lunch?

But on this day, while heading back to his office (which is in the White House) and traveling down the road, the politician's limo was suddenly cut off by some crazy greaser who was driving down the road in his 1950s hot road that was speeding like a maniac.

The politician's limo driver did not see the guy coming, and to avoid an accident, he had to make a fast reaction, so he jerked his wheel really quickly and the next thing that happened was the limo went into an uncanny fishtail.

There he was, the fat old politician white Politian who cared for nothing but money, is not getting thrown around the back of his limo and physically bouncing off of the door like a human ping-pong ball and is fearing for his life. The old money hungry politician had not though of money while his life was flashing before his eyes.

After what felt like five minutes of pure terror, the limo finally came to halt is it went crashing up onto the curb. The sudden stop of the vehicle then made the politician fly forward and he then smashed his head on the front glass/divider, and it nearly knocking him out.

Amazingly, the limo driver and the politician where not hurt in the incident and they pulled themselves together and got out of the limo to make sure everything was okay, and as soon as the politician foot hit the ground and he stood up, he then pointed his finger at the car that just cut him off as it was speeding away and yelled out loud, "HEY, that guy was aggressive driving!" The politician then went back to work at the White House, told everyone what happened, and the word aggressive driving got put into the system.

Too bad the greaser and his aggressive driving did not run the lame but powerful politician who cared for nothing but money right off of a cliff. Then the words "aggressive driving" would have never been invented or put into the system.

Also, my justification for hating this word is this. When you get pulled over for aggressive driving you don't get an aggressive driving ticket, you get a reckless driving or careless driving ticket (Reckless, four points; careless, two points). Just give me an aggressive driving ticket and give me six points, Officer, would ya! It would make more sense to me, but then again, what would a Road Rage ticket be, ten points?!

And to date, the only state that actually has a Road Rage ticket is California. You go California. It is a six-point ticket so I would not do any Road Raging in California if I were you.

I thought it would have been New York or New Jersey that would have invented that ticket, as it is a known fact that New York and New Jersey has more traffic violations than any other state in America. When it comes to Road Rage incidences such as accident and collisions, most major cities have high numbers just as you would expect just because of a higher population of people, rather than smaller less populated states.

When and Where Did Road Rage Start?

Well, for Christ's sake, that is a hard question. And I am just going to give you a quick chop shop (sum up) to answer it. I could write a whole chapter on this on question alone. It probably started when the first road was ever invented or made, and who knows when that was, really?

If you want to go back to the beginning of time, they were first called paths. Jesus walked the path of righteousness, not the road, and for the most part, a path is for walking purposes only, not driving.

Then there were trails. A trail is just a bigger path that leads from one point to the next, but trails are not man made and do not have a smooth plain. Only way to refer to it is like them dusty trails that the cowboys and Indians used to travel on with horse and carriage. That is why we used to play that game as kid called the Oregon Trail, and it was not called The Oregon Road! But I bet there was a lot of trail Rage back in the days of them cowboys and Indians. I can see Wild Bill yelling now, "You better get your horse off my trail, you stupid Mohican, before I shoot them feathers right off your head and make you look like a bald, beakless turkey!"

Then there is the word "roads," finally! And this is the real definition of the word road.

Road: A long or narrow stretch with a manmade paved or smoothed surface that leads from one point to the next and is made for traveling on by motorized vehicles such as cars, motorcycles, etc., or by natural resources, horse, carriage, bicycles, etc.

Because roads are so old experts are unsure of the origin of the word "road" itself. Most think it came from the Middle English word "rode," meaning "a mounted journey." This may have come from the Old English word "rad," or from the Latin word "ridan," meaning "to ride."

For some reason I read the meanings and the origin of the word and did not understand it at first myself. So I made an example story so I, and maybe even you, can better understand how this word was originated.

Example Story: Picture it, there once was a Latin man walking down a road. As the Latin man is walking down the road, he notices an Old English man riding a horse carriage coming toward him. The Old English man passing by notices the Latin man walking also, so he decides to stop and then ask the Latin man if he needs a ride. So the Old English man then asks the Latin man, "Hey, do you need a rad today, sir?" and the Latin man replies, "Do I need a what?" Then the Latin man says in return, "I was going to ask you if you could give me a lift down the ridan!?" And then Old English man replies, "A lift down the what?" and then two travel together and talked and they found out that their words meant the same exact thing.

Now, if you want to discuss the first roads ever made then we got to give it up (give props or recognition) to the Egyptians. They were the first man to make a smooth surface road with stone markers, and leading from one destination to the next nearly 2000 years B.C. It is funny to think that the only things traveling those great first roads were, people, camels, and possibly spaceships. What, you never read *Chariots of the Gods*, by Erich Von Daniken?

Next is a toss-up, really, as some would say that these guys are really greatest road builders ever, and those were the Romans. These guys laid a solid base and gave the road a pavement of flat stones. The Romans also knew that the road must slope slightly from the center toward both sides to drain off water. This gave the road what is called a crown.

The Roman road builders knew also that there must be ditches along the sides of the road to carry water away into some of the first ever drainage systems. Roman roads were built mainly to get soldiers from one part of the empire to another. These roads ran in almost straight lines and passed over hills instead of cutting around them. The Romans built more than 50,000 miles (80,000 kilometers) of roads in their empire and some of them still are in use today.

Then coming to America around 1500 A.D. The first early Americans settlers lived in the wilderness. There was nothing here yet but new land to build on, and them Indians. They built and established their homes along the rivers and bays and used the water for transportation. As new settlers went inland, they usually built crude roads (or trails that them early pilgrims made) to the nearest wharf. Until after the War of 1812, people traveled mainly on foot or on horseback through trails, as mentioned before, the Oregon Trail game.

But the first real and extensive hard-surfaced road was completed was not done and completed until 1794. This road was called the Lancaster (Pennsylvania) Turnpike. Praise the Lord, the first real American road. It measured 62 miles (100 kilometers) long and was surfaced with hand-broken stone and gravel. Hand broken, you say, no wonder why our forefathers were so tough! Who said that the Flintstones were really that primitive? They may have been a family that existed only a few generations ago, not thousands of years ago.

Over the next forty years, many more turnpikes were built. Most surfaces were of earth, gravel, or broken stone. Some roads were covered with logs or planks which were laid crosswise. Where logs were used, the roads were called corduroy roads. Both corduroy roads and plank roads were very bumpy. From 1830 to 1900, there was little change in the surfacing materials for roads and highways.

Then there was the railroad. It was the first thing built that was a smooth man made surface that was made to travel on by the first motorized passenger vehicle, the steam locomotive. Imagine the sight of that big beauty. The first steam powered railroad locomotive debuted on February 21, 1804. On that day the engine/train carried and moved ten tons of iron, five wagons, and seventy men nearly ten miles in four hours and five minutes. Crazy, I know. I think I can walk ten miles faster than that train did those miles, I just don't think I will be carrying that type of weight, though.

So take off the rails of the tracks some odd ninety years later and you have a smoother road. Just around the same time the first cars were being built from the 1890s through the 1900s. And also around the same time nice roads of cobblestones were being built in big cities like New York and Boston.

This was the up-and-coming era of the road, the highways, and the motorized vehicles all at once! It got bigger and progressed all through the 1910s and 1920s. I am sure Road Rage was roaring through the 1920s also just like everything else was, as hence, why they called them the Roaring 20s. You had big cities, congested living areas, scarce resources, and now traffic on the road and no real order to it all yet.

Example Story: Picture it, a guy is speeding in his brand-new 1915 Cadillac through a busy intersection in Michigan in the year 1915, and as he speeds by he nearly runs over a man who is crossing the street. The man walking that was almost hit yells to the man driving the Cadillac, "Hey, jerk! You almost hit me because you just blew through that stop sign!" The guy driving the Cadillac stops his car immediately, looks at the man walking, and replies back, "What in the hell is a stop sign?!"

That was the time and place the first stop sign was invented and placed in the United States, in Michigan in 1915.

So you can only imagine how bad Road Rage and other road problems, such as parking, turning, speed limits, and even just trying to enjoy a Sunday ride must have been back then before there was any real order to it all.

So in America from the early 1920s up until the present day, beautiful paved roads, black-top highways, turnpikes, tunnels, bridges, and whatever else you want to throw in there have been being built at a nonstop rate, and have been growing every day since them first pilgrims came to this beautiful land that we now call the United States of America.

What has also been growing in that time is the number of cars, trucks, busses, taxis, traffic laws, lights, signs, and rules to keep the mass populations under control as it grows.

So, as it stands, even though roads were built thousands of years in Egypt and Rome before America, we have by passed (or paved right over) everyone else in history. America as of today, with all its youthfulness and being younger then almost every other country, America is now the king of the highways and byways and has more roads cutting through its territory than any other country! God, knowing that makes me proud. We have more Road to Rage on than anyone else in the world. Nice to know we truly are king of the road!

And with that note, we also have some of the first Road Rage incidents ever recorded and will take the award on this one also for the question of: When and where did Road Rage start!?

"Road Rage" appears to have been coined in the USA in the 1980s. Several citations of it exist from that time and place, for example, this from the St. Petersburg (Florida) *Times*, 2nd April 1988:

"A fit of 'Road Rage' has landed a man in jail, accused of shooting a woman passenger whose car had 'cut him off' on the highway."

A rival newspaper, the *Ocala Star-Banner*, ran the story on the same day and they included a quotation from a police officer: "'It was just a traffic incident that sparked the whole thing,' Police Chief Bob Roberts said of the shooting. He said the suspect had [a] simple case of 'Road Rage.'"

It doesn't seem likely that the "prisoner" coined the term "Road Rage," but the enclosing quotation marks around the phrase are an indication that it was already known, but not necessarily known to all the paper's readers, in 1988.

How Is Road Rage Doing These Days?

In fact, in the past decade Road Rage has gotten so bad that psychologists have actually classified it as a mental disorder for certain people. They say, many drivers who are prone to sudden emotional outbursts, or inappropriate reactions are now said to suffer from what is called Explosive Intermittent Disorder.

Excuse me, miss, come again? Did I hear you correctly? So what you are telling me is that one hundred of New York State drivers, 95 percent of New Jersey drivers, 75 percent of Los Angeles drivers, and

80 percent of Boston drivers all suffer from Explosive Intermittent Disorder? No S***!

Well, you better hurry up and make a pill called De-Rage and give it to all these folks who have Road Rage 'because you can make some bank (capitalize on it and get rich), you corrupt politicians. Imagine how many pills you would need to cover all those people with Road Rage. You would need at least five pills a day for every person that drives.

You know what would be perfect for this situation also. I would love to hand out a bumper sticker to everyone that has this condition saying, "I suffer from a horrible case of the Explosive Intermittent Disorder, buddy. Now back off!"

Is this crazy? Yes, of course, but you know what, they have a name for every disorder under the sun these days. Really all the people have to seek is some good anger management classes or get some counseling, grab a stress ball, and chill the hell out. Not be diagnosed as something and then have to take a pill for it. That just makes people believe they are sick and that they will have to stay that way.

Is Road Rage Funny?

I would have to say that it depends on the person doing the Road Raging and the situation at hand! I know when I see a short, fat, old, bald guy, or an old lady Road Raging that poses no real physical threat, yet they are screaming out death threats, it can be funny as hell.

There is nothing funnier than seeing and old women who is driving in her 1956 Chevy Impala stick her hand out of her window, extend her middle finger, and then tell the person who is a quarter their age that is driving next to them to "go F… yourself!" It makes me laugh to the point where I cry a little bit every time.

But a Road Rage altercation can be very serious and not funny at all when there is someone potentially dangerous doing the Road Raging. The last thing you want to do is get into some Road Rage battle with some ex-con (someone who did time in jail) who is bald, is seven feet tall (though you can't tell their height till they get out of their car to kick your ass), weighs more than the car he is driving, and his name is Bubba. Usually you bump into them in jail, not on the road, but hey, you never know, someone may have bailed them out of jail and lucky you were the one to catch them out on the road and decided to yell at them. Good luck getting out of that one.

You get into a Road Rage altercation with someone like that, you will be wishing that you hadn't because the way it always ends is them pulling you out your car and slapping you around a little bit.

Are There Types of Road Ragers?

I am glad you have asked this question. Why yes, yes, there are types of Road Ragers. You know, anyone can be a Road Rager. From a soccer mom, to a taxi driver, to your grandmother if she is having a bad day and decides to flip you off. Anyone at any time as long they are behind the wheel of a car and are angry enough and that they decide to show it to another person can be a Road Rager. But the fact of the matter is that most people don't do it very commonly, like your grandma. They do it maybe once a year when they are having a bad day on the road and decide to show the proper hand gesture, and then they won't do it again for years.

But there are common forms of Road Ragers that are very noticeable, actually. I have compiled a list of all these Road Ragers and put the names of them also so you can notice them next time you see them on the road so you can try to keep your distance from them, and inevitably protect yourself.

And I am 100-percent certain you have run across one, if not all of these very common types of Road Rager forms that most people take on, that is, if you have not taken on the role of one of them yourself before! Read the list and enjoy.

Regular Road Rager - A Regular Road Rager is your most common form of Road Rager. It is just a regular person, usually your soccer mom, having a bad day and taking it out on the rest of the world from the front seat of her minivan! They have been under a lot of stress and today is the day that they will let everyone know about it.

They like holding their horn down (or better known as the blow-off valve) just to let us all know that they are upset, and they might cut you off in a rude manner and speed inappropriately if you hold them up today. They are angry and the only way they feel that this tension will be lifted is by getting to their destination faster by moving you out of the way if need be.

This Regular Road Rager will do this today because they are so upset, but they might see them do it again for four years.

Road Lunatic - This is the most severe type of Road Rager. This is the person you see a few cars ahead of you nearly causing an accident and making a scene in midday traffic.

Example Story: Picture it, you are a forty-year-old white male, who is on the way home from work, and you are a car insurance agent mind you, and while driving up the highway in your 2000 Silver Ford Mustang, you all of a sudden notice another car ahead of you swerving their car at other cars. As you question what the hell is going on, you take a closer look and then you see a person now throwing stuff at people from their moving vehicle as they are driving down the highway, and as you gasp, you look and then this person sticks half their body out their car window and they start yelling and waving their hand, "COME ON!" This person is trying to entice other people to fight with him right there in traffic. You move over to the next lane that where traffic is moving, so as you get over, you then speed up as to pass this person and as you drive by and look at this person, you witness a crazy person having a massive fit of Road Rage.

As you drive by you say to yourself, "Wow, look at that guy, he's is a lunatic!" and then you laugh a little more and say, "I'll swill still give him a good quote on his car insurance, though," and then you continue on home. Hey, insurance agents always need to make that sale.

Road Lunatics are the type of people that carry a golf club around in their car and it is not for golfing. Their cars usually have A LOT of dents and/or broken windows from many Road Rage altercations, so be on the lookout.

Road Bully -These are different. Road Bullies are Road Ragers that come in larger form most of the time. Road Bullies come in big trucks with heavyset blue-collar men driving them. They only pick on you if you are the driver of a smaller vehicle. They are bigger; therefore, they are better. That is their mindset. You know, kind of like that big bully jock high school mentality.

If you try to pass his Dodge Ram 2500 in your little Hyundai Prelude you might get crushed, and it won't be by accident. They only let other big fellows pass first. The bigger have the right of way in their eyes, and those are their rules so you must abide by them.

Road Snob - A Road Snob is a fancier form of a Road Rager. They use rude behavior to upset other people. Road Snobs always come in nice cars. They are better then you because they own and drive a brand-new white BMW or Mercedes Benz, like anyone cares what you drive. Oh, yeah, and they are always talking on that damn cell phone like they are special or something.

Example Story: Picture it, there you are, you are a fifty-year-old Italian dude and you are driving home from work, which is a land scrapping job and you are in your 1987 Ford F-150. As you are driving down the road coming home from work, you begin to see a car ahead of you that is coming out of a mall shopping center, and it looks like they are going to come out right out in front of you. This person ahead of you is not supposed to do this, as it is a double yellow line, but as to not cause an accident, you slow down and then stop and let the person go anyway even though you don't have to. If you had hit them, it would have been their fault! But the good man that you are avoided that.

So as you come to your halt, you see this really nice brand-new white BMW with some hot chick driving it that is on her cell phone that is right in the middle of the road. You wave your hand out of the window as it is okay for them to go and pass across the street and go the other way, and as the car takes off, the Road Snob DOES NOT WAVE BACK. They did not acknowledge your kindness what so ever. That is your typical Road Snob, they love make the wrong turns, they love to drive a better car than you, and they love to insult you. The person did not wave back to you because you were in a shitty old pick-up truck. Had you been in a new Mercedes or BMW like her and you were a hot guy, then she would have waved back.

Road Punk - Road Punks are what you would call in your everyday life a Young Punk. They are the new teenager drivers that drive around town and have NO respect for the road and the other people on them. A Road Punk will run your grandma down if she gets in his way, and that is if she is driving or walking!

He is you next-door neighbor's Young Punk kid. He just bought a used 1996 Camaro off of Craigslist, and you know how you have been hearing the punk is his father's garage late into the night making noise, that is him putting on an even louder exhaust pipes just so he can piss people off and provoke them into racing with him on the road.

Oh, yeah, and he will also be coming home at 2:00 A.M. drunk this weekend and peeling out up and down the street just for the fun of it.

His room is a mess and he has no job if you like to know the full extent of his uselessness and carelessness.

Road Hog - A Road Hog is a person who usually takes up two lanes when they are driving on a two-lane road! They usually drive a massive 1976 Ford LTD and it takes them three lanes to turn their car like a tractor trailer. Also, they do not drive over 22 miles per hour ever, not even on the highway. This is your typical Road Hog from back in the day. Old men like our grandfathers used to drive what we used to call boats around, not cars.

But the Road Hogs of the new millennium are kind different. Now they have H3s (a watered-down Hummer), Range Rovers, and huge Ford Excursions. Are more so than not, they have little housewives driving them. I know, some two-foot-tall lady really need a Ford Excursion. The new Road Hogs pull up in front of Shop Rite and take all three of the parking spots that are left, and please don't try to park near them because they can't drive those big trucks for shit, and on their way out of those three parking spot they will hit and dent your parked car, and they won't even know it and they will leave.

Oh, yeah, and did I forget to mention that when they drop their kids off at school they stop DEAD in the middle of the road, they and do not use hazards, and then let their kids get out on both sides of the vehicle!

Road Demon - You can call them Road Demon, but they are better known as Speed Demons. Road Demons are just people who get a thrill of going fast. They do it all the time and nothing will slow them down. Not even when they have one of those donuts (small spare tire) on their car that they are not supposed to be doing over 55 miles per hour with it. You still see people doing over 85 on the highway with those suckers on. How those tires don't pop and they don't crash into a wall, is beyond me.

Also, if you are driving and you get passed by a Road Demon you will know it. It will be like The Flash just went past you so fast that it scared you and you almost wet your pants. And when that sucker passes you, you will hear something also. It will be the music of Sammy Hagar, song name "I Can't Drive 55."

Road Scumbag - A Road Scumbag is a person who drives a car that is so beat up that it should be in the junkyard, and not on the road. If they live in New Jersey or New York, then they are probably paying more for car insurance a year than the actual car's worth. That is if they even have any car insurance.

A Road Scumbag knows that their car is worth nothing so if you try to pass them in your nice new Benz (Mercedes Bens) they might just hit into you 'cause they got nothing to lose, baby. They know your car is worth more, so don't even try it.

Their car is usually a Dodge Aries (K car) or Ford Escort 1992 and below. Other signs also is that their cars burns a ton of oil and has an exhaust leaks. You can usually smell and hear that road Scumbag coming from a mile away, so look out.

Chapter 2

Do You Have Road Rage?

If you are reading this and already said *NO!* to the question "Do you have Road Rage?" then you have a problem. The problem is that you are lying to yourself, and you are living in what is called denial.

"Oh, yeah, and how do you know that, smarty pants," you ask? I know it because you, me, and everyone who has ever lived and has ever used a motorized vehicle on a road has had a Road Rage outburst at least once in their lives. No one can change that and there is nothing you can do about it. It is kind of like a universal law or something. If you drive, eventually you will Road Rage.

Do we like to admit that we have Road Raged before, or that we do it every once in a while, of course not, it makes us look bad? But if you have a problem with Road Rage that is persistent, you do it more than a few times a week, or have a case that was as bad as mine, I Road Raged every time I even get into a car, then you must admit to yourself that you have a problem and try to get help for yourself like I did.

Or you can live in denial just like I did for twenty-six years and yell at your friends and family and say, "I don't have Road Rage!" while you have a speeding ticket in one hand and a careless driving in the other, and just let the problem get worse and worse. Yes, I know, blame it on everyone else who is on the road, including the cops, and not yourself.

For example: I was just like Cole and Rowdy from the movie *Days of Thunder*. By far, one of the best movies ever made. Especially if you actually liked crazy car movies from the 1980s and 90s growing up just like I did.

There is the part in the movie when Dr. Claire Lewicki (Nicole Kidman) says to Cole (Tom Cruise), "YOU and Rowdy have the same sickness; it's called *DENIAL* and it's probably going to kill you both!" That is the best statement a sick-minded Road Rager like myself could ever hear.

So for sticks and giggles, and to truly help you decipher if you are a true Road Rager or not, I have come up with something that will give you a good solid answer to the question "Do you have Road Rage?" and to determine just how bad it is!

I have come up with a Road Rage Test that will actually tell you how bad your Road Rage is. Imaging that, finally an answer to why you have gotten into so many Road Rage altercations in your life.

The Road Rage Test goes over a lot of things. It goes over how you think, how you act, how you feel, and how crazy and dangerous you actually are. After you answer all the questions, add up all your points, check the scoreboard, and it will tell you just how bad your Road Rage is.

The Road Rage Test consists of fifty total questions. Forty of the questions are in a Yes or No section, and ten of the questions in a multiple-choice section.

For the Yes or No part of the test, give yourself 1 point for answering Yes, and 0 points if you answer No.

For the multiple-choice part of the test, give yourself 3 points for answering A, 2 points if you answer B, and 1 point if you answer C.

At the end of each test add up your answers, then add both test answers together for a full result. For example: If you answered Yes to all forty Yes or No questions and A to all of the multiple-choice questions, then your score will be a total of seventy points, which is the top score.

Part 1: Yes or No Questions

1. Have you ever yelled things out of your car window when stuck in traffic like "Come on already!" "Let's go!" or "Move your car out of my way, A** ****!"

   Yes   No

2. Do you think riding someone's ass (tailgating) is a way of saying, "Get out of my way, slowpoke!?"

   Yes   Noo

3. Do you think old people should not be allowed to drive on the roads, AT ALL?

   Yes   No

4. Do you have a no# 3 sticker on your car?

   Yes   No

5. You are sitting there waiting at a red light. As soon as the light turns green, are you the first one to beep at traffic if it does not starts move right away?

   Yes   No

6. If someone cuts you off on the road while you are driving, do you feel the need to cut them off in return worse or retaliate in some way?

   Yes   No

7. Have you ever been stuck in traffic and thought of the woods or sidewalk as a way out? And I don't mean parking your car and walking. I mean actually thought about driving through the woods or on the sidewalk!

   Yes   No

8. Have you ever thrown something at someone else's car, from your car from your car while driving? Like coffee or pocket change?

   Yes   No

9. Have you ever break checked (stepped on your breaks on purpose in order for the person behind to rear end you) some because you thought they were driving too close to you and that they deserved that?

    Yes   No

10. Have you ever giving someone the finger or any other rude hand gestures while driving?

    Yes   No

11. Have you ever driven around for more than a week or two with your check engine light on in your car? Or you actually put tape over it to forget about it completely!

    Yes   No

12. Have you ever thought of your car as a weapon? Or actually used it as one!

    Yes   No

13. Have you ever passed your exit, street, or turnoff that you were supposed to get off at to actually continue a Road Rage altercation with someone else? As in chase someone down!

    Yes   No

14. Have you ever pinned out (made your car go as fast as it can) your car for more than thirty seconds through midday traffic hoping that people will just move out of your way? And if they don't, screw them anyhow!

    Yes   No

15. Have you ever passed another motorist on the right when you were not supposed to?

    Yes   No

16. Have you ever borrowed your parents' car? And crashed it!

    Yes   No

17. Do you believe the speed limit on the roads in America should be at least 100 miles per hour? And maybe 125 in the fast lane!

    Yes   No

18. Have you ever gotten into a physical confrontation (had to get out of your car and fight) because of a Road Rage altercation?

    Yes   No

19. Have you ever pulled up right next to another driver that you did not know, and yelled obscene things at them because the way they were driving upset you, and you had to let them know how you really felt?

    Yes   No

20. When you are driving and see a yellow light at an upcoming traffic light, do you tend to hit the gas pedal instead of the brake pedal?

    Yes   No

21. Have you ever gotten mad while you were driving and punched your steering wheel or your dashboard?

    Yes   No

22. When you see cars that look fast driving down the road (Mustangs, Corvettes, Hondas with stickers on them) do you try to race with them?

    Yes   No

23. When you are sitting at a red light, do you actually look at the opposing traffic light to know when your light is going to change? And that it takes three seconds from when the other traffic light turns red for yours to turn green, but I bet you already knew that.

    Yes   Noo

24. Do you take it as personal insult if someone cuts you off when you are driving?

    Yes   No

25. Does it hurt your feelings if the person next to you has a better or faster car? And you think that he/she is stuck up and does not deserve that car?

    Yes   No

26. Do you carry a stress ball to squeeze when you are driving around?

    Yes   No

27. Have the cars that you have owned personally (not the ones that you have borrowed) been so beat up by the time that you were done with them they were not even able to be resold? You had to send the cars right to the junkyard!

    Yes   No

28. Is your car not even reusable for scrap parts by the time you are done with it?

    Yes   No

29. Have you ever gotten so mad when you were driving that you had to pull over to cool down because you thought you were going to explode?

    Yes   No

30. Have you ever been stuck in traffic and wished you had a monster truck named Bigfoot so you could use it to run right over all the cars in front of you?!

    Yes   No

31. Has your car ever broken down, and when you were pulled over on the side of the road, you got upset at the car and kicked, punched, or tried to hurt it in some physical way?

    Yes   No

32. Have you ever run another driver of a vehicle off the road with your car?!

    Yes   No

33. Has someone ever beeped their horn at you when you were stopped at a light or somewhere, and because they beeped at you, you got so mad that you actually got out of your car to reprimand them? Meaning, get out of your car, walk up to their car, point your finger in their face, and say, "You beep that horn one more time, and I am going to break your hand!"

    Yes   No

34. Have you ever been stuck in traffic and flipped out in a fit of rage and grabbed your steering wheel, and jerked back and forth violently! You know, just like Bruce Nolan (Jim Carrey) did when he was stuck in traffic in the movie *Bruce Almighty*?

    Yes   No

35. Do you think every stop sign should be a yield sign? Or do you actually treat them that way anyway!

    Yes   No

36. Does your car make funny noises (loud muffler, pinks and pangs, stuff rattling around, screeching belts, or other funny sounds) from all the abuse that you put it through?

    Yes   No

37. Do you carry weapons with you in your car? Especially right next to your driver's seat!

    Yes   No

38. Does your weapon have a nickname and black duct tape wrapped around it?!

    Yes   No

39. Does your car have missing pieces (bumper, muffler, fender, handles, glass, ext.) and you still drive around in it?

    Yes   No

40. Do you think you are king of the road and that everyone else

who is on the road when you are driving should move out of your way, and if they do not they should be thrown in the dungeon and treated to a life of torture for such behavior?!

Yes   No

Part 2: Multiple-Choice Questions

1. If you are stuck in traffic and someone is trying to merge from an/a entrance right into your lane, you:
a) don't let them in. Period.
b) hesitate to let them in (huff and puff), then finally do let them in when you realize you have no choice.
c) wave them right in, like you owe them a favor.

2. You are driving down the highway at full speed in the left lane (65 miles per hour) and someone starts tailgating you and flashing their lights at you to make you make move. You:
a) jam on your brakes to slow that mother down.
b) stay in your lane and let him find his own way around.
c) get into the middle lane and let them pass, and you mumble, "Go ahead, jerk."

3. You are on your way to work and you get stuck in dead-stop traffic (you know, you woke up late and left thirty minutes later than usual), and when stuck inside your car, you:
a) start to get frustrated, beep the horn, and actually get out of your car to look ahead at the traffic and think of using the emergency lane to get out.
b) start using your stress ball, and fiddle with the radio.
c) you put the seat back, chill out, and call someone.

4. You are driving in traffic and a car stops dead in front of you to let someone out at a store or something. This is a one-lane road so you cannot go around. You:
a) lay down on your horn like it is a weapon, and curse them out

for stopping like that.

b) beep twice to try to get their attention and make them move, and don't say anything verbally.

c) just wait until they move, and when you drive by you notice it is an old man letting his wife out in front of a store and you smile and wave and so does she.

5. You go out for a Sunday ride. You are driving and minding your own business when you get cut off by someone and they give you the finger because you were going to slow. You:

a) chase them down and do the same thing to them, and maybe give it to them worse.

b) get behind them and beep the horn, and high beam to piss them off, and then turn off.

c) you just let them go and laugh it off.

6. You are in a hurry to get somewhere because you are running late. So in your rush you accidently cut someone off. The other person gets mad, starts beeping and yelling at you, and starts to follow you and threatens you to pull over. You:

a) grab your Louisville Slugger and get ready to pull over and bust someone up.

b) take off at a high speed and try to shake them off, cutting through traffic, and speeding down side roads to lose them.

c) try to get their license plate, call the cops and report the person, or try to find a police station to pull into.

7. You are driving around and you have a couple of Road Punks throw a can of Red Bull at your car and try to egg you on to race them. You:

a) say to yourself, "I'll show these Young Punks!" and start to race with them and throw something right back at their car.

b) race with them for a while until you pass a cop going way too fast and slow down and pray and hope that you don't get pulled over.

c) just turn off to avoid the whole thing.

8. It is 8:55 A.M. and you just left your house to head to work. You were supposed to be at work at 8:00 A.M. You:

a) get into your car (forgetting to do your hair and brush your teeth, looking like hell), and fly to work at Mach 3, cutting everything off (even cops) to get to work. And when you pull up at work, it kind looks like the scene from the movie *The Chase* with Charlie Sheen. At the end of the movie when they pull up at the border and there are one thousand cop cars, five helicopters, and border patrol behind you.

b) get ready properly but still speed to work.

c) just call the boss and tell him you are going to be late, take your time, and put no one in danger because you are late for work.

9. You are on your way to work and already in a bad mood because of your wife. All of a sudden, as you are stopped at a light, some-one bumps into you and you are involved in a fender bender. You:

a) get out and flip out at the other person, calling them profani-ties, and give them an even harder time because you are really mad at your wife and not them, but they are going to get it.

c) get upset, try to stay calm, but when cops show up blame the whole thing on the other guy.

d) just get out, be respectful, wait for the cops or switch insurance, and go your separate ways.

10. You are driving down the highway and you are coming up to a set of tolls. The line for the tolls is about one mile long and takes you twenty-five minutes to get to them. As you finally get to your exact change toll there is one more person in front of you. You get stuck behind the dude looking for change for like five minutes in his car! You:

a) ram that jerk's car with truck and push him right through the tolls!

b) just beep and yell like everyone else, "COME ON! MOVE IT!" *BEEP-BEEP!*

c) just wait patiently until they go through, or you try to back out and go to the toll over from the jerk.

Chapter 2: Scoreboard

The "Do You Have Road Rage?" Test Scoreboard

You answer score can range from **70 points**, which is the highest, to **10 points**, which is the lowest. The higher the score, the worse your Road Rage, the lower the score, the better off you are! This is where we see how *Raging* your Road Rage actually is. So, let's see what you got!

70-65 points: Let's not sugarcoat this one. Let's put it to you like this. You are the Adolf Hitler of Road Rage. I am sure if you could kill/execute everyone who upset you on the road, you would without even blinking and eye. I know you would.

And I am just as sure that you would also like to be able to drive to work in one of those nice German fire launcher tanks like the Nazis used to burn cars, trucks, and just about anything else on the road that got in your way.

You don't have Road Rage. You have some deep-rooted psychological disorders and you should have that checked out pronto. They may need to lock you away for a long time and give you electroshock therapy.

64-61 points: You Road Rage is Code Green. "What do you mean by Code Green," you ask? Your Road Rage when you get mad is probably more dangerous than if we even put the Incredible Hulk at the peak of his anger behind the wheel of a car.

And in this case, I am also sure of one more thing, that when you are mad and you are about to start Road Raging, that you actually wish you could do to cars what the Incredible Hulk could do to them! Tear them in half with his teeth and chew them up and spit them out.

If I am on point (right about what I am saying) so far, then I bet your Road Rage is so bad that you even drove your bicycle dangerously when you lost your driver's license for the third time. Some people never learn. How many states is your license revoked in again?

If this is all true, as it is for me, then you should seek professional help for you anger issues before they end up getting you hurt, or worse yet, you end up hurting someone else because of them. If I could recommend anyone to deal with the major anger and Road Rage issues you have, I would recommend a personal session with Anthony Robbins. He might be the only one skilled enough to handle a case as bad as yours.

60-55 points: Your Road Rage has just one wish. You wish that you could be able to drive that Mustang from the movie *Death Race* and your local roads and streets legally! Part of that wish is that you are able to use all the weapons on it also and destroy everything in your path at all times when you are Road Raging. That sounds like a lot of fun, if you ask me.

Since you scored this high, then I am also certain that every one of your cars that you have ever owned and driven has been sent to the junkyard when you were done with them because you beat and abused them to hell. And I also bet at least one of your cars has caught on fire somehow, by accident or not!

You are still pretty sick in the head, you pyro maniac. Maybe you got hit in the head pretty hard when you were younger just like I did and there are some screws loose? You should get to some anger management, and seek out a doctor who specializes in people with pyro problems.

54-50 points: You are still a true Road Rager! If you put on a mood ring (those ones that change colors with your feelings) when you are driving and you get into a fit of Road Rage, the ring would glow hot red and melt off of your finger.

If you scored this high, then I bet you have at one time or another thought about moving to Germany, and it is not because you have relatives there (you are half German/half Irish). It is because there is no speed limit on the Autobahn and you want to go as fast as you want all day long without anyone giving you a hassle about it.

There is only one doctor for a guy like you. Dr. Seuss. You need to laugh more often and stop taking things so seriously, really. That is why you are always in such a bad mood and so mad. Stop letting people on the road piss you the hell off and get over it.

49-45 points: You Road Rage is still pretty bad and you are still a hothead! I am sure you have punched your dashboard a few times in your day when you were upset. Be careful, a cracked dashboard lowers the price of the car.

I bet you even carry around things to purposely throw at people's cars if they upset you?! Yeah, we all know, the best thing to throw is pocket change. It makes a crazy loud sound when it hits their car, and it won't really break anything or kill anyone. It will just scare the living daylights out of them. Or half-filled water bottles fly the farthest if you are going for distance!

If you are doing stuff like this like I use to throw things from your moving vehicle at other ones, then maybe instead of going to see a shrink (psychologist), you should go seek help that maybe a pitcher from a baseball team might see if you like to throw things, like a coach.

44-40 points: Sure, when someone upsets me on the road also all I want to do is go all *Dukes of Hazzard* on their ass to and pass them like I own the road and leave them in a cloud of dirt and smoke, all while yelling, "YEE-HAW!"

If you scored this high, then I am certain that you have definitely thought, if not tried for real, off getting your own personal car to fly through the air just like good old Bo and Luke used to do every day in that gorgeous *'69 Dodge Charger* called the General Lee. I know, it would be amazing to live like that, wouldn't it? Fast cars, outrunning cops, girls in short shorts, and yelling YEE-HAW all the time? Good times. There is no known cure for the Dukes of Hazzard syndrome, so I am sorry.

Once a cowboy, always a cowboy.

39-35 points: Okay, so last time someone cut you off you through your coffee out of your window at them out hoping it could catch them in the face and it would burn their eyes out, forcing them to not see so it would send them into a fishtail and then cashing their car. Hey but you were having a bad day, no big deal. You don't do that type of stuff every day, only around that time of the month you do.

Seek out a doctor to put you on the right medication for that man-o-pause.

34-30 points: Your Road Rags is not too bad, Mad Max beyond Thunder Dome. You are really starting to cool down and take it easy on the road these days. Yes, you had 44 points on your license when you had that 1978 hot red Camaro and a mullet back in the hay days of 1988. And yes, you used to cruise up and down the avenue all night thinking you were the man, messing with people and trying to race them. But you don't go out of your way to mess with people on the road anymore, and that is a good thing. You are getting to old for that. Your glory years of Road Raging were twenty years ago.

Unless! someone messes with you on the road, though that is a different story! It takes a lot to set you off, but like other diseases, Road Rage can lie dormant for many, many years and it can come back out of remission at any time. If it comes back out of remission, then you may have to start you anger management classes again to put it back into it.

29-25 points: Your Road Rage is on a normal level. Not too bad at all. So you got a few speeding and careless driving tickets in your day, big deal. Everyone gets those. You are definitely not no Dale Earnhardt of the public roads (like everyone who has a no#3 sticker on their pickup truck). Public road Dale Earnhardts can be a very dangerous form of Road Rager and you have to look out for them.

You may just have gotten carried away while driving down the highway and listening to your loud rock-and-roll music and keeping up with traffic, so you go into the zone and you ended up doing 85 miles per hour and then got pulled over for it.

24-20 points: You really don't have Road Rage, mister. I let everyone pass me by on the road as if you own them a favor. You maybe got into one or two Road Rage altercations on the road in your whole life, but I am sure you are not the one who even started the situation. The jerk behind you did.

You may have an outburst or two of the Intermitted Disorder once in a while, but you definitely do not need to seek out any special help or counseling for it. Well, you should seek some help for your marriage that is going down the tubes and your gambling problem, but that is a whole different story, right?

19-15 points: Road Rage does not even pertain to a person like you. You are a soccer mom or maybe even a schoolteacher and the last time you got mad was when your kid did not listen to you because you told them not to watch too much TV.

You don't get mad at people on the road because you have better things to do with your time. You only get upset when you are late to drop your kids off at school and you are stuck in that line of one hundred cars and that is it.

Isn't it amazing, though, how you can pull up at a school fifteen minutes early and there are two other cars, but if you pull up five minutes before the bell rings, boom, stuck there for a half-hour? Eighty-two percent of Americans runs late.

14-10 points: You are a saint, not a soccer mom. You have no points on your license and you have never even got pulled over in your life or even yelled at anyone for driving stupidly.

The only one who should score 10 points on this test is the Pope or Jesus Christ himself. And that is because these men never drove! Well, I don't know about the pope if he ever drove or not, but I tell you what. If I put Jesus in a brand-new hot red Mustang that can do 150 miles per hour and stick him in traffic for two hours with it, I bet money that he would get upset after a while, feel it is unfair, and get mad and punch his dashboard and start yelling, "GODDAMN IT," OOPS, sorry, Dad.

If you really did score this low on the test the only thing I can say about you is this. You have a good head on your shoulders, and patience! You don't act like most people on the first thought that comes to their mind, or the first feeling that comes rushing through their body. Yes we all get mad in our little boxes we call cars, and in our little boxes we call homes, and in our little boxes we call heads. But it is all on how you act out on that first emotion or feeling. If you can control that first emotion and recognize it for what it is, just a feeling, you will be able to control it and control anything else. If you want to control something in life, control the thoughts and emotions of yourself, and don't worry about someone else. If you just keep trying to control what other people do on the road and everywhere else in life, and take the focus off yourself, you will get angry, and you will have Road Rage and be angry for the rest of your life. Plain and simple.

Chapter 3

What Brings Out Road Rage in People?

First and Foremost: A Bad Attitude and Anger Issues!

The first main offender that causes Road Rage and I am sure everyone already knows this, is a bad attitude combined with some anger issues. It is known that 75 percent of dangerous Road Ragers have a bad attitude or anger issues in their lives to begin with before they ever even got into a car.

People with bad attitudes and anger issues are mainly the type of people that take their anger and frustration out on everyone in their lives, not just people on the road. They do things like take their anger out on their spouses ("When are you going to pay the damn bills, honey?!"), their children ("Do your homework now, you little S.O.B.!"), their coworkers ("If you come in late to work one more time you are fired"), their neighbors ("Get your garbage can away from my house, scumbag!"), and now YOU on the road ("Get your car out of the MY way, A******!").

They have a bad attitude and treat most people like S*** in their lives because of it, and they also resort to using anger to make other people feel bad so they can feel better about themselves.

So if you already have a bad attitude, and you walk around every day with a chip on your shoulder, and things seem to anger you quite easily, and both are upon you in that same or current moment, and then you decide to enter your car, the percentage that you are going Road Rage at another person when you are driving is basically at 100 percent. The only way you won't Road Rage is basically if there are no other drivers on the road, and it is just you! Hopefully you are driving somewhere in the middle of Alaska, but even then, you might run into an ice road trucker!

It is almost unavoidable for a person like yourself to avoid Road Raging. So, put your bad attitude aside and swallow your pride, my man; you will go nowhere in life fast if you yell at people.

Second in Line, Snobbery and Selfishness
Something else that people get into their heads that brings on Road Rage is selfishness and snobbery. It is the things that we say to ourselves in our heads like **"*Me* first"** or **"*I* was here first"** and the **"They have to move out of *MY* way!"** and **"*I* am in a rush!"** And this is just a few of the things that we say to ourselves in our heads that invoke our selfishness.

And now, once we start to say things like this to ourselves, and we combine them with the power of belief, and we believe that **WE** or **I** are supposed to have the right of way first, and we don't get it, boom, all hell breaks loose and you start to Road Rage.

Feeling like you are supposed to get something first, or be treated a certain way, expecting certain things, is a selfish way of thinking. We set ourselves up because once we don't get treated the way were expected to be treated, like we are some kind or royalty, we react in a rude manner and snobbish manner.

And how does this Road Rage come out, we flip out and we start yelling things at other people on the Road like **"*I* was here first and you need to move your car out of *my* way!"**

Example Story: Picture it. You are a thirty-five-year-old white female who is single, and you are getting ready to go on a new date tonight with someone that you met off of *Match.com*, so you going to the mall in your 2005 VW Rabbit so you can go shopping for some new boots.

When you get there, you pull into the parking lot and you start driving around looking for a parking spot. After a few minute, you see no open parking spots, so you look over into the next lane over, see an open spot finally, so you gasp, and then you floor your car and you start driving through the parking lot at 100 miles per hour and race for it.

You come around the turn into the lane in which the open spot is with your tires screeching, and as you fly down the lane and you get to the parking spot you, your eye brows lower and anger comes upon your face and you see that another car getting to the open parking spot at exact same time that you are.

And as you expected, you both try to pull into the spot at the same time to fight for it, and you almost crash into each other. Next, you both get out of your cars and a fight brakes out over a parking spot! You start yelling at each other verbally, "I was here first, jerk!" "No, I was here first!"

Next thing you know, boom, and you punch (yes, a woman punching a man) the other person in the face in a fit of Road Rage and you knock the man clean out. They go down like a sack of potatoes, and then they start yelling for the cops as now they are playing the victim game, and then you run to your car and take off like a bat out of hell. You go, you bad girl you. You may be tough, but you will be wearing an old pair of boots on that date tonight.

So, let me ask you. Do you think that you were the one in this case who was being selfish, or the other person? If you said the other person, then you are half right, because you were both wrong and being selfish. People have to use blinkers, and they have to drive the speed limit in the parking lot. The other person may have been driving the speed limit which is 15 miles per hour, but you were doing 100 miles per hour, so in all, they did deserve it, but screw them, right.

Bad Company, or Also Known as a Backseat Driver

Another thing that can bring out Road Rage in people is not the other drivers on the road in their cars, but none other than people traveling with you in your car!

Man, there is nothing that I hate worse than a backseat driver, let me tell you. And I am sure everyone else in life hates it just as much as I do.

And isn't the backseat driver the usual suspect, some old crazy family member who stuffed right behind you in the back seat so their voice pierces your ear, and then they start yelling at telling you how to drive, when to turn, and that you should slow down because you might kill them. And then you yell out, "Hey, DAD, if you were so worried about getting there in one piece, THEN YOU SHOULD HAVE F****** DROVE!"

Example Story: Picture it, it is a Sunday morning and you are a middle-aged white family man who is driving his family to church in his 2005 Ford Taurus station wagon. Good man that you are.

But as usual, you are late for mass because the family has a tough time getting themselves together in the morning, so on your ride to church you start driving a little fast as to make up for some lost time and trying to rush because you are running a little late. You hate to walk into anywhere late, as it is embarrassing.

Your father (the man who looks like the dad from *Leave it to Beaver*) is in the back seat and he immediately gets upset because of the way you are driving, so now he has to throw his in two cents (his stupid opinion) and of course, he starts yelling at you and telling you how to drive. Mr. Beaver yells out, "Slow down, son, look out for that guy, turn right, look out yellow light, and SLOW DOWN, or we are going to see God a lot sooner than I expected!" You cringe as he yells at you over and over again.

You get upset, but you don't say anything. Everything is ok for a while, but then you speed up again, and the old man starts right back up. Now the man does not shut up and he keeps on talking and talking and as he does you can feel your blood start to boil! So now, instead of driving slower, you start to drive faster and crazier and you don't even realize it because you are so mad. The anger is going right through your body, down your leg, and down through the gas pedal, and your adrenaline is now fueling the engine, and it is like racing fuel.

Now, as your speed increase, so does your father voice, and your father gets even louder and yells again, "SLOW DOWN! YOU ARE GOING TO KILL US BEFORE WE EVEN GET TO PRAISE THE LORD TODAY!" Then you reply, "SHUT THE HELL UP!"

Your mother, who is also in the car, gasps at your language and almost faints. Then she says to you, "My God, son, has the devil gotten into you!?"

Then you all start to yell at each other and it turns into a full-out verbal argument and you have to pull over to calm down. The devil did not get into you, but that Road Rage sure did because of your backseat driver, Mr. F***G Beaver, who never knows when to shut the hell up!

Others backseat drivers can also be your friends that do this kind of crap to you. It does not always have to be family, even though they are the best at pushing your buttons.

Also your girlfriend/boyfriend can always put a damper on the way you drive and become a backseat driver. Only problem is that they are usually in the **front seat,** so it makes matters ten times worse.

Your beloved partner knows how to push your buttons pretty good also. They agitate and upset you just by asking you those same stupid questions over and over again in that nasally annoying voice, like, "Did you really have to take that turn like that?" "Why are you driving like this?" or "Why are you going so fast?" "Why don't you slow down?"

Most of the time you just want to reply with a formal, "Why don't you just shut the F*** up!" Mind you, they ask you these same questions every time they are in the car with you, and know the way you drive, and know that asking these stupid questions upsets you, yet they still do it every time they are in the car anyway. I know, stupid.

It is just like the same stupid questions that they ask you in the morning to irritate the hell out of you and ruin your day, like "Why do you slurp your milk out of the bowl after you eat you cereal?" My ex-girlfriend used to ask me that question in that nasally and annoying voice and it used to burn me up (get me mad), yet she had eaten breakfast with me a million times, and knew that I did that, but she still had to question why I was doing it?

You know what it is with some people, it is just that they are annoyed with themselves at that particular moment and they have nothing better to do so they just chose to bother and irritate someone else to make themselves feel better. That is all that it is, nothing more. They like to waster their energy because they have nothing friggin' better to do, so don't let their stupid-ass questions upset you.

Best solution to the backseat driver is by a car, and rip all the seats out of it except for yours and drive around alone so you don't have to listen to anyone's crap anymore.

Driving with a Hangover

A normal thing that brings on Road Rage is your A** waking up late from being hungover because you drank too much the night before and had too much fun. Why is this a problem? Because when you try to do anything hungover, like drive, like talk, like work, like eat with a hangover, or even function normally, it just does not work out okay for you.

We all like to sleep late when we are hungover, and then try to do everything normally but it does not work out like that unfortunately. We always end waking up late and having to try to get ready in a hurry, eat in hurry, and try to get to work in hurry by driving 500 miles per hour all while hungover. Feeling like we are going to vomit, feeling sick, having major brain fog, and having a massive headache.

When you are hangover also, you are like a five-year-old girl that just got her ice cream taken away from her, moody and cranky. Why are you cranky and moody? Because you did not have time to take a shower, you did not eat your breakfast, you are really dehydrated, you are sweating out the alcohol from the night before, and today is the busiest day of the weak at work, of course. We always seem to just get a little too drunk the night before we have some major things going on in our lives. Don't we?

Example Story: Picture it, you stayed up until 4:00 A.M. to party with your boy Robert. Hey, it was his birthday and you guys have been friends since college. You had to be there for him, and take all those shots with him, of course. You couldn't let him drink alone.

So after getting home at 5 A.M., and then falling asleep, or actually passing out from a drunken comatose, you missed your alarm and you ended up waking up a little late, twenty-five minutes late.

You wake up, peeling your head from the pillow that is fool of drool, look at the clock with one eye open, because the other one is sealed shut with crust, and you then jolt out of the bed and you try to get your S*** together in a flash.

You don't even wash your face or brush your teeth, and you literally through your clothes on your back, and then you run out of your house and jump into your car and take of like a bat out of hell (really fast) to try to get to work on time.

As you speed down the road, you try to put your tie with one hand, and the with the other hand you pick up your cell phone call to call your secretary to tell her that you are going to be late. How many hands do you have again? As soon as your secretary answers, you start yelling at her, "SARA! I will be late for my meeting, tell them to wait!"

As you fly down the road well over the speed limit, you try to piece work your hair together in the rearview mirror, one cowlick at a time! So now you are speeding down the road multitasking (talking on the phone, doing your hair, doing your tie) and now you are not even really looking at the road or paying attention anymore. Fantastic attention you have when you are hungover, no? So, as we all do when our minds are not focused on the road, we drive right through inspections in which we were supposed to stop at, but of course we don't because our minds are somewhere else.

And guess what, as you crossed the intersection without looking you almost hit and old lady crossing the street. By the grace of God, you looked up just in the nick of time to see her and swerve your car out of the way, just missing Grandma Moses. Though, you missed her, you didn't miss the curb as you turned the wheel just too much in your state of panic plus hangover, and your car hit a curb instead and you just blew out your tire.

After your tire blows out your car swerves and you lose control and then you go off the road and land and come to a stop in a patch of grass. While this happen, you nearly S*** your pants in the process.

Now, you get out of your car and then you start to yell at the old lady and calling her stupid old bat for being in the road, even though she had the right of way. In return, the old lady tells you to go screw yourself, laughs at you, gives you the finger, and then she continues on her merry way.

You should have stayed in bed, my friend. Driving with a hangover can be really dangerous. Especially when you have a bad case of the brain fog. We don't think or act as accordingly as we usually do when we are in this state of mind.

We are angry, moody, can't think straight, feeling ill, want to go back to sleep, want to vomit, and now we are trying to drive faster than we normally do when we don't have the brain power to focus on the road while we do so?! Not a good idea if you ask me. If you want to avoid a case of Road Rage and want to keep from hitting curbs and blowing out tires, don't drive when you are hungover, trust me on this.

Being a Control Freak

Another thing that brings on Road Rage on is control issues, or being a control freak as some would say. Yes, we know that you love to be in control of everything all the time. But the road and how people drive is something that none of us, except for maybe cops, have any damn control of and it sucks.

You are going to run into people on the road no matter what you do in life and they are going to drive as slow as they darn well please, or however fast they darn well please, and there is nothing that you can do about it unless they are breaking the law. And the only thing that you can do is maybe grab their license plate and call it in (call 911 and report the offense), and wait for the cops to catch them, which the cops most likely won't because they are at the donut shop. Besides that, you have no control over what other people on the road are doing, especially if does not involve you.

Yes, I know you have yelled out the window over a million times in the past at people telling them what to do, and saying things like "Drive faster, slowpoke!" "Move your car out of my way, A******!" "You can't park there, dumb ass!" and the most famous, "SLOW DOWN BEFORE YOU HURT SOMEONE, JERK!"

However, as much as a control freak that you are, it was not your place then, nor will it be in the future, to say anything to anyone when they are doing something wrong on the road unless it truly is endangering your life or someone else's.

It is fact that as soon as you yell at someone, and you tell them what they are supposed to do, and if you are not an authority (boss, parent, cop) and you are just a regular person, either they won't listen at all, or you will get back a rude response. And then once you get a bad response to your unlawful command, get what is going to happen, thing will go from verbal too physical in a flash because we all know how you respond to rude behavior, Mr. Controlling.

Yes, I know you tell your kids what to do. Study hard, kids. Don't misbehave in school, go to bed on time, shut off the TV, and no more computer for the night. Yes, I know you tell your spouse what to do also. Hey, honey, don't wear that, wear this; don't eat that, eat this; don't buy that, buy this; don't put that there, put that here; and the most famous, don't screw me like that, screw me like this!

In fact, you are such a control freak that I bet you even tell your own parents what to do now that you are older. Don't do that; you'll get hurt. You are too old to move!

And what, you thought I forgot about your work life, Miss. Manager at Starbucks? You tell everyone at work what to do also. Hey, guys, do this, do that; clean this, clean that; stock this, stock that; make this, make that; wash this, wash that.

But guess what now, everyone you know has always listened to you, I am sure. Maybe they do it because they admire you and look up to you, or hey, maybe they just do it out of plain fear. And yes, you do get far in life with a confident, kind of bossy, controlling attitude, this is true, but when it comes to the road, you have no control. I am sorry.

So when it comes to you telling other people on the Road what to do, forget about it, because if you get back a negative response to you command, and the person does not do what you said, such as slow the hell down, you will want to go after them, and a Road Rage altercation will take place. So refrain from telling other people what to do on the road at all cost, no matter how much you want to, and you will avoid many road rage altercations. And when it comes to people telling you what to do on the road, God forbid, just take it with a grain of salt and listen to the person, even if you don't want to, until they are no longer visible, then do whatever the hell you want.

Taking Your Anger Out on the Wrong Person
A lot of us, when we drive around from place to place is probably one of the only times in life that when we actually get to spend some time alone, so we get time to think and sort out our thought. Unlike at home, at the office, on the job site, at school, and even at the bar, where always have someone chewing our damn ear off because people always need to talk.

So often, when we are driving, we get to spend that little bit of alone time that we need to think about things. Now, "Are the things we have time to think about when are driving around good or bad," you ask!? Well, that would that all depend on what you are thinking about.

I know a lot of us go into deep thought when we are driving around alone. It happens to everyone; we all have a lot on our minds. There is only one problem, though, if what we are in thinking about in our minds has a lot of bad in it while we are driving around. This can lead to a situation.

I know this sounds crazy, but some people in fact would say that driving around is kind of nice and actually relaxes their mind. Imagine that. Some people even go out for what are called joy rides! Something a true Road Rager like I and you would know nothing about. They like to drive around and take that time to think about nice things and relax.

How on earth is that possible? I don't know, because that almost never happened to me when I would go out driving.

But then there are people who go into a bad place in their head when they drive around alone, often, like you and me. A lot of people do this. They tend to think and dwell on more of the bad things that are going on in their lives when they are driving around than the good. Their time that they spend with themselves alone in the car is no good!

Example Story: Picture it, there you are, you are a forty-year-old bald white dude that works as an accountant for a living, and you are diving home in your 2004 silver Toyota Camry that is a tiring sixty-minute ride to work and home from work every day. God Bless you, the things you do to provide for your family. Each day you can't help but to go into deep thought when you are driving. Anyone that drives for that long would. Heck, most of the time you are probably just think-ing and it seems like the car is driving itself.

As you are driving home from work next thing you know and you don't even realize it, boom, you are in deep thought and are having a full on argument with you wife in your head about something that hap-pened yesterday. You replay the terrible events about that argument that you and your wife had over who burned dinner! You took the blame in the argument even though you were not wrong, but it was only to shut her up. Now this taking the blame over dinner situation replays over and over in your mind and you think how you could have won the argument if you could have just said something different, like "If you had set the timer, this would not have happened!"

As you are driving and thinking about this situation in your head, you got all bent out of shape and upset over it. You are actually getting mad about this problem with your wife that is not even real at the mo-ment and that happened yesterday, and now you are driving around in a bad mood because of it. Yes, this has happened to me a million time. I end up mad about something that happened yesterday.

Next thing you know as you are driving in this unrealistic bad mood, some poor fellow who is driving tries to get over into your lane and comes just a little too close to your car. Boy, do I feel bad for him.

Now, you are no longer thinking about yesterday's problems, but now you are focused on the one in front of you, and it is this poor guys that cut you off, but the anger from yesterday is there today, and it is going to be going that guy's way.

Next, you end up beeping your horn at the guy in front of you and then flipping out. You then drive right up next to the guy and start cursing him off to all high hell, and just as he turns to look at you to see what in the hell is going on and who is Road Raging at him, you say something extremely odd and funny. Grasp this, in the middle of your Road Rage fit and cursing this poor man out, you actually called this chap your wife's name and you yelled out what was in your head. You said, and I quote, "I didn't burn the Goddamn dinner, you B***H, YOU DID! Now watch it!" The person you are Road Raging at hears you, and the gives you a cockeyed look back and pretty much knows that there is a madman yelling at him because he knows nothing about burning a dinner.

That guy that got too close your car and got Road Raged at by you got what is called *The S*** end of the stick* that day. He got somebody else's anger spewed out all over him.

You see, you were mad at something completely different that was not even a real situation at the moment, and then you took it out on somebody else on the road who did not really deserve it. Either that guy was in the wrong place at the wrong time, or your head is just always in the wrong place when it is in your car, and that my friend is the wrong time to let your head go there. So don't take you anger out on the wrong people, especially on the road, it is just unhealthy, and go so seek some psychology help and some marriage counseling, pretty please, before you end up yelling at someone else on the road to take out the trash.

Mindset or One-Way Street

Something that I like to think brings out the Road Rage in certain people I think are mindsets, or known as a frame of mind, a certain way you think. One mindset, or frame of mind, most people know about and have is called a one-track mind! Come one, I know most of your parents have this mindset. Listen, you have known them for the last twenty-five years that you have been alive, and they have not changes the place that they eat every Friday night, the house that they live in, the way they talk, the way they walk, their job, the way they eat (they slurp their soup), and they still talk with a broken accent even though they came to this country forty-four years ago, and they always tell you to do the same thing, your friends are bums, and you should get a job. So, what makes you think they ever will change?

Hey, they did not get this far in life by being open-minded, so leave them be and stop trying to change them because it isn't going to work, trust me on this.

But the mindset, or frame of mind that I think brings out more Road Rage in people is what I call a "one-way street" mindset, but other that know it would refer to it as having "a narrow mind." You only see things one way, and it kind of works like this.

I can do something on my street, drive a certain way, but you cannot. Basically, I used to believe that just I, and only I, could speed down my street because I lived on it, and if other people used to speed down my street I would yell at them and throw things right at them for doing so and tell them to never do that again. Hey, I have lived in the same house for basically thirty-five years, pay my taxes, and pretty much out stayed most of my neighbors. I put my time and money in, Goddamn it. I believe I own the whole street by now, for Christ's sake.

Example Story: Picture it, you are a twenty-four-year-old, tall, white Polish kid, this is driving home from college in your 2003 red Kia Sorrento, and you are in one hell of a bad mood.

You are rushing to get home to relax, and as you are nearing the finish to get home, as soon as you make the turn to get onto your street, you punch the gas petal and you start flying down the street at full speed and you are heading for home like a rocket.

Now, as you are flying down the street, that same courteous neighbor Jeffery who is always out in front of his house and doing his stupid lawn work again, which he loves to do more than his wife, turns his head as he hears something roaring down the street like a dragon, and as he looks up he takes a notice that it is you racing down the street, yet again.

You are going a little too fast (95mph in 25) so Jeffery, the courteous neighbor that he is, worried about the neighborhood children decides to yell at you while you are flying by, "SLOW THE F*** DOWN, ASS****!" This is not the first time he has done this, nor will it be the last.

Did you happen to hear Jeffery as you were speeding by, of course you did, so you rolled down your window, stuck your head out, and you retaliated back at Jeffery with a "F*** YOU, OLD MAN! DO YOUR YARDWORK AND SHUT THE F*** UP!"

You don't give two S***s about Jeffery. You don't care for his attitude, for what he said to you, and sure as hell done like his lawn. In fact, you are thinking about pouring some of your old motor oil on it in the middle of the night just to get back at him for yelling at you like that.

So nothing becomes of this situation between you and Jeffery, because it has happened before and it will happen again, no big deal, but something else happens.

A week later your mother asks you to cut the lawn at home. Karma's a mother, right? Lawn work is something thing you are not too fond of doing, but you are in your mid-twenties here, and still live at home so you really have no choice in the matter. So you head outside to cut the lawn.

There you are, on a nice Saturday afternoon, hungover, cutting the lawn in 100° weather (but it is New Jersey and it is humid out as usual, so it feels like 120°), you are sweating bullets, and you are kind of in a bad mood because of the situation.

Now, as you are cutting the grass you see someone you don't like coming down the road. It is that damn kid Esteban that you hate so much from school. He is coming to pick up his girlfriend, that young eighteen-year-old hot chick from across the street that you like to look at from your bedroom window with your binoculars. And guess what, Esteban isn't going to slow, either; this jerk is racing down the street, he is peeling out, and he is beeping his horn!

Now, you don't like Esteban for a few reasons. One, he likes to beep his horn every morning when he comes to pick up his girl and wake your ass up. Two, he is younger than you. And three, he just came speeding down your street! You say to yourself, "How dare that little son of a bitch speed down my street!"

He has done this before and you have not said anything, but being you are already hungover and in a bad mood and sweating you B***'s off, you will have to use your anger to advantage and have it be the fuel for motivation to say something today!

You shut down the lawnmower and start walking up to Esteban's car as he pulls up. You yell as you walk out into the street, "Hey, punk, you better slow down when you come down *MY* street! And you better stop beeping your horn when you pull up here in the morning! You got it!" and you walk right up to his car. Esteban replies and babbles, "Yeah, sure, bro, whatever you say!" and he ignores you.

Now, your hot neighbor girl comes out of her house and he gets into his car. You get even more upset now about what Esteban, and this kid is completely ignoring you, so now you lean into his window to go and grab him and choke the living hell out of him, but just as you lean in the window and you grab hold of his shirt, boom, he hits the gas and start peeling out in your face and he takes off to get away from you!

You yell as he takes off, "Stop it A** H***, I am not done with you yet!" Esteban yells back to you, "UP YOURS!" and as he peels out in your face and leaves you in a cloud of blue smoke and gives you the middle finger!

There you are, feeling just like how you made Jeffery (the courteous neighbor) feel. What come around goes around, I guess. But how can you get mad at someone for doing the same thing that you have done, and will still do? You can't! You don't have to do anything or listen to anyone, just as much as they don't have to do anything or listen to you. So your "one-way street" mind says this: "I can't do what I want, and no one can tell me what to do, and I can tell people what to do, and they have to do what I say!" I am sorry, but "the rules of the road" or "the laws of the universe" do NOT work like that, Mr. One-Way. So if you want to avoid Road Rage altercations, take one of Jesus quotes into consideration, and do unto other as you would have done unto you. Don't speed like an animal on other people's streets if you don't want them to speed down yours, because it is a two-way street.

One Word: Provoking

Another good one that brings on the Road Rage is provoking! This one has always been my favorite. This works both ways, of course. Whether it is someone busting your balls (bothering and provoking you) or you are bothering and provoking them, it is something that can get people to go right into Road Rage mode. You have got to be careful who you provoke, though, because you could provoke the wrong person and they might not like it.

Some times on the road you might get away with provoking certain people who are timider than others and you might get away with doing things like, riding someone's ass (tailgating them), beeping the horn excessively, and plain out yelling at people, this is true. Sure, you might provoke and scare some people with your Road Rage and get them to move out of your way, but you might also provoke the wrong person and you might get your ass handed to you (get you beat up) if you are not careful, or it could get you in a lot of legal trouble. Cops don't like it when they see people provoking others as it is rude, dangerous, and can cause an accident or a fight.

Example Story: Picture it, so there you are the other day, driving to the mall (you live in New Jersey, there are one hundred malls, pick one), and you are driving in your nice new—wait, sorry—certified pre-owned 2006 hot red Mustang. Yeah, it is a pretty fast car, but you are a thirty-seven-year-old white man that never worked on cars, you went to school to fix computers, and your wife owns your bank account, and your B****S, and you are not a racecar driver, so you are just a normal guy that never speeds, or are you?

So you are driving to the mall on a two-lane highway that has traffic lights on it. As you are driving, you see a red light ahead and start too slow down, and then come to a complete stop. As you have been driving down the highway to the mall, though, you noticed something odd a short time ago. You noticed this beat-up black car of some sorts tailing you (following you) for a few miles. You become a little curious as to why this car has been driving so close to you, so you keep an eye on the car as it comes closer to you see in your rearview.

As you are now completely stopped, you look in the rearview and see that the car that has been following has disappeared. You get a little nervous and happy, hoping that the car may have turned off, but just as you turn your head, your hopes are smashed to pieces as you see the the car that was tailing appear to your side. As you look over, the driver of the vehicle that was tailing you decides to pull up right next to you. You know trouble is upon you as the car now starts revving its engine to get your attention. You look over buy just by moving your eyes, not you hole head, as you are still a little too scared to move your neck yet. Fear has part of your body paralyzed.

You look over, with just your eyes, and you notice two young hood-lums (people that look like trouble who possibly live in the ghetto) in a 2001 Honda Crx with a grapefruit shooter exhaust on it looking to race you! The two hoodlums start mouthing off and provoking you to you to get you going (to upset you)!

They start yelling, "Hey, old man, you know how to drive that thing!" and then they start to laugh at you. They say, "What is that, an automatic, bet you can't even drive stick, loser!" "Let's see what you got off the line!"

You don't even say anything, of course, because you are too intim-idated and you really are driving an automatic, so you feel like a sissy, and you can't think of a comeback to say because you have not been verbally abused like this since you divorced your ex-wife.

But now, they keep on going and going, and the provoking is start-ing to really bother you, and you don't like that. Now, you are insulted as the one kid just called you a "B***H" because you aren't even looking at them. Now you feel that your pride has been hurt and it is at stake here, you feel anger and rage build up, and you are going to have to do something about this mess.

So what do you do, you decide to give it a shot and race with the young hoodlums. So you rev your motor, and get into position so when the light changes to green you can take off. The hoodlums laugh at you again and start edging their car forward.

The light turns green and, boom, the Honda and the hoodlums takes off like a BAT OUT OF HELL (really fast) and their car sounds like a lawnmower on steroids flying down the highway. They leave your ass in the dust and give you the finger as they pull away. Bad move on their part giving you the finger.

So you could have let the whole situation go, but no. Their vulgar provoking has hurt and pride so much now that you are beyond mad, and now you have become furious.

So you decide to play catchup with the hoodlums and after five minutes of speeding and weaving through traffic (not smart) you catch up to them stopped at a light. You stop your car at the light also, put it in park, and get out of your car and run up to theirs on foot. The hoodlums see you running up like a crazed maniac and get scared and roll up their windows just in the nick of time so you can't grab them. You pound on their window, nearly breaking it, and look like a rabid dog foaming out the mouth that is trying to kill them. The human Cujo has jst come to pay them a visit.

The two hoodlums get scared and start to scream like little girls and then they floor it and they take off before the light even changes. They almost cause a huge accent as they fly through a red light, and you are standing there in the middle of the road and everyone is looking at you because you are the one who pretty much provoked that into happening. Yes, you almost re-provoked a major accident.

The hoodlums did not know you had that wild side and they provoked the wrong person that day. Yeah, you may be a simple man who lets women run and ruin his life, but you only take shit from them because you love them, not from other jokers (unserious people).

When some people are provoked and insulted like that, whether on the road or not, in country slang, they don't take too kindly to it! And it can get you hurt real fast.

Don't provoke people unless you think you are able to handle the consequences that come along with it, because it can possibly get you beat up.

And if you are provoked, don't let it bother you. You have to learn to swallow your pride, no matter what is being said to you, and you have to let it go. If you scream at, Road Rage at, or throw fists at people if someone who provokes you, just like you did back to the Hoodlums in return, in the end, it is only you who end up looking bad because the people that usually start the provoking are the ones who turn into the chickens and taking off, like the kids in the CRX. Real people don't find the need to bother others. And you could have avoided that whole Road Rage altercation very easily by just turning off, and not letting their provoking get to you. By you going back at them and retaliating, it almost caused a serious accident when they ran through that intersection, and had something had happened, you would have been in serious trouble,

Problems Letting Things Go

One of a Road Rager's biggest problems that is related to why they get into so many Road Rage altercations that always end up escalating into more than just a beep of the horn is because they have major problem letting things go!

Yes, that is right, you heard me. You have a problem letting things go, buddy. And that is even in the smallest of arguments and fights. If you claim to be the true Road Rager that you are, then I am sure that in even the smallest of arguments that you have had on the road with people have turned in your stomach for weeks and you may even have ulcers because of them.

If you don't believe me that things eat you up when inside if you don't learn to let them go, just ask me how many times I had to get my gastric system checked out at a young age, as I had to go for an engiscope scope twice by the age of twenty-six to be check because I always had so many stomach problems. Turns out, those stomach problems were not coming from what I was eating, it was directly related to what was eating me: Holding onto too much **Anger** for too many years because I never let anything go.

When you have a problem letting things go, this can cause a major problem for you on the road because every time you go out driving and someone gives you the finger, or yells at you on the road, you will always the one who takes it to the next level! I know how you are.

This is the primary base a person's mentality who has problems letting things go, and this is you and I. When someone on the road beeps at you or gives you the finger you take it as a direct and personal insult, and the person who has done this to you must be reprimanded and punished for their behavior toward you and you cannot because they must learn their lesson and you must be one to teach it to them immediately. Yes, this is the way you truly feel deep down.

You cannot let go what they have done to you. They must have their feelings hurt worse in return because it is a matter of pride! And deep down it might make you feel better because you got to them last. What a childish attitude, don't you think?

Example Story: Picture it, there you are, you are a twenty-four-year-old Italian kid from New Jersey and you are on your way to the DMV of all places in your 1984 Ford Bronco II to get your driver's license reinstated after having lost it for a year (yes, you are driving at this current moment with a revoked license), and as you are driving down the road, all of a sudden someone beeps at you and gives you the finger because of the way you are driving. You were going too fast in the right lane and passed someone one the right improperly, so because of this the person you massed got mad, so they sped up and caught up to you to let you know that you did something wrong and how they felt about it.

Now after seeing that, you then say to yourself in your head, "How dare that SON OF A B**** do that to me, That B**** has got to pay for that!" You are not letting that one go, and right after you say those words to yourself, you floor your old piece-of-junk truck and then you start to chase the person down that gave you the finger (passing your destination, the DMV, because getting back at the person for giving you the finger is more important) and now you plan to give it back to them ten times worse in return, if you know what I mean.

You catch up to the person, and as you do you pull up right next them, and as they look over at you with a pissed-off look on their face, you give them two fingers instead of one, mind you, while holding down your horn with your elbow, and sending so much intensity through the wire that you almost burnout the fuse and start an electrical fire because you are pressing it so hard.

Now the person who you have insulted back, floors their car so they can get away from your crazy A**, and so you chase them again. There you are, racing down the road chasing someone down like a maniac, going over the speed limit, yelling out of the window and cursing, and not paying attention to the road because you are too busy looking at this person because your nervous system is in fight mode.

You end up driving over 90mph to catch up to the person you are chasing, in mad day traffic a might add, and as soon as you catch up to the person, you pull up alongside of them once again so you can really give them a piece of your mind. The person does not look at you because they are going too fast and he wants to focus on the road so he does not crash, but you however, are way to mad and you want to tell them that when they stop their car that you are going to kick their A**, and badly I might add, so as soon as you look at them and start to yell, the person jams on their breaks and they slow down immediately and you look behind you, and not in front of you like you are supposed to. And guess why he jammed on his breaks, not because of you, but because of what was ahead of him, and now you look forward and see what he seen, traffic at a dead stop. You should have payed attention to the rod buddy, because now you look forward at the last second, gasp at what you see, jam on your breaks, come to a skidding halt, and then you end up rear ending someone and getting into an accident.

"How did it end up," you ask? Luckily no one was badly hurt in the accident, and your air bag deployed, saving your dumb head and keeping you from getting hurt, thank God, right?

So no one was hurt badly physically, but you will be hurt pretty badly emotionally very soon as the pride that you set out to redeem in that fit of Road Rage is really going to get hurt even worse now, as the person who you chased down to Road Rage at just pulled up next to you, smiled, applauded your stupid behavior, and now just pulled away laughing at you! Go chase home down again. Oh, wait, you can't, because your car is stuck to someone else's.

Now you see, you could have just let the whole situation go, but no, you could not let it go, you have a problem doing that. Listen, buddy, when they flipped you the bird you could have just waved and kept on going and enjoyed the rest of your day and not even let it bother you, but your mentality is still very childish and you need to work on it a little bit.

Letting things go will save you a lot of grief in life, whether on the road or not. We only hurt ourselves by getting angry and not letting it go in order to keep our pride. Let it go.

Road Rage Buddha says, when someone gives you the finger, and you wave and smile back, the person who just tried to insult you know becomes the insulted.

Head Games and Questions

And no, we are not talking about the head games and questions that come along with a bad relationship, because God knows that we have all had them in the past, and women love to mess with a man's head just as much as man loves to mess with a woman's.

So, what we are talking about here are head games of the road. These are the mental games that we assume that people are playing on us on the road and then tend to make us upset.

But what I say is the part that agitates people the most is not always others questioning us, but it is the constant questioning that we do to ourselves in our heads about what others are doing to us, and why they are doing it that make us assume things, and then it makes us want to go nuts and want to flip out. Yes, we question ourselves into a state of crazy if you will! You have to remember something; people can't play head games with you if don't let them, buddy.

This is the plot. Many of us have been in a situation before were we actually had to question whether or not a driver on the road in front was holding us up, or going slow purpose just to piss us off, and when the questioned was answers with a, "Yes they are", then becauase of that answer we then drove up to the that person in front of us in a fit of Road Rage and we flip out on them and made a scene and they don't even know why. Yes, the person you just Road Raged at did not even know what in the hell was going on to begin with as they were just lost, as that is the real reason why they were driving to slow, but now they have you screaming at them and they don't even know why. So yes, it was the question as to whether or not this person was messing around with you on purpose, and then the answer to that question that made you act out in a fit of Road Rage that brought on this whole escapade of stupidity and false aggression.

Example Story: Picture it, you are a thirty-eight-year-old white woman who is driving in your 2002 Ford Explorer, and you are on the way to your sister's house for her baby shower. Yay, time to celebrate.

You are driving and you are already a half-hour late because of your kids, as usual. I know, my kids always give me hell to when it comes to getting ready and I have to be somewhere on time.

Now, as you are driving to your sisters house, your two kids who already made you half-crazy just trying to leave the house, now start yelling up a storm in the back seat, so to get them out of the car quicker and to get them to shut the hell up, you start hauling A** (driving faster) down the road to make up for lost time so you can get them out of the car so they will stop crying.

And, but of course, as soon as you decide to speed up and you are driving down the two-lane road a car decides to turn out of intersection right in front of you. They turn into the right lane of traffic that you are traveling and they go so slow that you have to jam on your breaks in order to not hit them. So this Jack A** now cuts in front of you and does not even move their car, so because of this you get really upset and then you begin to play the game of *20 Questions* with yourself.

- Why the hell would they cut me off like that?
- Why are they holding me up?
- Who would give someone like that a driver's license?
- Don't they know 1 am in a rush?
- Why won't they get out of my way or speed up?

So after asking those few questions, you get just a little mad, because the answers are never good, so you beep the horn at them, but you get no reaction from the driver in front of you. So, because your horn has no effect on the dead beat driver in front of you and they will not speed up or wake up, you then decide to switch lanes so you can try to go around the person who cut in front so you can go your way. You quickly put on your blinker and move over, and as soon as you get into the left lane, boom, the slow poke driver goes over into the next lane also and they stay right in front of you.

You both go over into the left lane simultaneously and now you have no choice but to stay behind them because the flow of traffic is moving in the right lane, and you can't get back over. Now you get even more upset and begging to ask yourself the bigger and more frustrating questions.

- What the hell is the matter with this A** H***?
- Don't they know how to drive?
- Don't they know the speed limit is 55 miles per hour on this road and not 25 miles per hour!?
- Why won't they move over?
- Holy S***, where is a cop when you need one?

You ask yourself all these questions in your head! And as you do you, you begin to feel your pulse starting to race now and you are getting really angry now, because you can't find an honest answer.

As you drive and think of a way out, you see a breakup ahead as your intersection is coming up that you have to make a left turn onto it to get to your sister's house. So as you drive along and pray for your intersection to come up quickly, and as it gets close by, you then put on your blinker and go to make the left turn onto the one-lane road, and as soon as you do, boom, the car in front of you goes the same way and they turn down the street in which you were going to first!

Now here come the questions that are going to make you start to get a little crazy.

- WHAT the hell is this, a F****** escort!?
- What, does this jerk know where I am going?
- When the hell is this person going to get the hell out of my way!?
- Is this really happening to me right now?
- How come this happens to me whenever I am late?

Now, as you both turn onto this one-lane road, you are now forced to stay behind this slowpoke for about another three miles, as that is how far ahead the next turn off is to your sister's house is, or any turn off is actually, so the slow poke in front of you can't turn off either. Life has given you three miles in which you must be patient, so as you travel along this road, you try as much as possible to keep your cool, but as soon as you hit the first half mile marker in your three mile journey, your kids start screaming so loud in the back seat that it rattles you to the core. You have no idea why they are belching out screams like this, and you can't handle it from the front seat, so this put pressure on you. You have no choice but to wait, so you try to calm your kids by playing some music.

Mind you, the person in front of you is still going 35 miles per hour in a 55-mile-per-hour zone, but you only have a half a mile to go and one more turn onto another road before you get to your sister's house.

You go to put on your blinker and make the right turn coming up onto your last road before your sister's house and as you do, boom, the person in front of you does the same thing! They make a right turn right onto the road where you are going. Yes, now you have two more miles behind them honey, so try to stay calm, but I bet you won't if these questions run through your head.

- Why does God always curse my life?
- What did I do to deserve this today?
- Maybe I should have stayed home.
- How can I get around this jerk?
- Is this person is doing this on purpose!

And after asking yourself *20 Questions* you give yourself the answer. You say, "That is it, I have had it, YES this mother F***** is doing this on purpose!" and you start to lay down on your horn and flash your lights at the person and nearly run them off the road because you are so mad. You get right on their bumper with your car and almost hit them. You start screaming with you head out the window and say, "Get the hell out of my way now, you SON OF A B****!" One of your little kids in the back says, "Mommy, stop it, you are scaring me!" but you continue on with your Road Rage escapade because you have had it with this jerk in front of you.

The person in front sees some crazed maniac right on their bumper, so because of this they go to pull over to the side of the road because of what you are doing, as to let you pass, and before they can even get halfway off of the road as to get into the emergency lane, you floor it and you fly by nearly running them off the road because you are pushing your gas pedal all the way into the engine compartment. Oh, yeah, and as you drive by you give the driver of the other car the finger!

Who was in the car in front of you, even though you don't give a shit at this point, it was just some little old lady that was just driving along minding her own business and was not doing any of this to you on purpose, nor trying to mess with you or your head in any way. You did all this to yourself in fact. That old bat did not even know you were behind her until she heard the factory whistle and then seen the grill of a Mack Truck, your truck, right in here rear view mirror nearly trying to run her off of the road.

Now don't you feel bad, as you just gave a little old lady the finger and nearly killed her, and you put your family in danger? Who cares right? It is all good (okay), as it is all over now as you're two miles past them and you have left them in the dust, or is it!?

Now, and finally, you can take a breath of air, and you just pulled into the driveway of your sister's house, and as you do you come to a screeching halt and then you jump out of your car as to let your frantic kids out of the car.

As you go to help your kids out of the car, guess who comes rolling up in the driveway right next to you as you are standing there. Good old Grandma in the car that was in front of you the whole time that you nearly just killed on the road. Guess who Grandma is, she is your sister's neighbor, that is why she was going the same way as you, knucklehead. Now go run inside and hide your face now, but guess what, you don't have time to, because now Grandma pulls up, stops her car, and give you one of the nastiest looks from the inside of her car, and she isn't breaking stare, either. She has dealt with your kind many times before.

So, next time you are driving, stop asking yourself so many questions like that. You are only going to make yourself nuts by doing so! You have to remember something, when you ask yourself something, you need to come up with and answer to be satisfied, and if the answer is negative, or you can't fine one, you will start to feel very uneasy. Just like when you asked that last question, "Is this person doing this to me on purpose?" and then you thought about it, and answered, "YES!" You gave yourself an answer, but it was the wrong one. She was not doing that on purpose. She is just an old bat that is just driving. She did not even know you were behind her until you tried to park your car in her trunk.

I hate to say negative things about anyone, but this can only help you in any case, and it is this. Some people in life are so oblivious to who they are or where they are, that if you think that they are in your way on purpose, nothing could be farther from the truth. Those type of people are what we call floaters, and you just have to be patient until the float away.

What Is the Bottom Line?

After reading this chapter I bet it got your blood pumping because it brought up so many fond memories on the road. And I am sure that you have been in some, if not all of these situations in the past just like I have, and have let these moments bring out the worst in you.

But out of all the situations that I can create, all the problems I can make up, and all *Example Stories* that I can write, whether mental, physical, spiritual, real, or non-real, there is a bottom line to the way that we react to things, whether on the road or not. What is the bottom line, you ask?

The bottom line is this. You react to certain situations in certain ways, because you are feeling a certain way, a certain emotion at the time. Yes, certain situations, conditions, and circumstance, that we are in at times make us feel different emotions and feelings, but if we cannot identify or control those feelings and emotions at the time we are feeling them and do something about it right away, next thing you know, boom, you are flipping out and Road Raging like a maniac, and the emotion has taken control of your body.

And just to let you know and help you identify these feeling feelings and emotions, they actually have names, and they usually tend to show up, or you fell them in a certain order also.

- Anxiety
- Fear

- Irritation
- Frustration
- Anger
- Rage

Example Story: Picture it, you are a thirty-year-old white woman who works as a secretary in a law office, and you are on your way to work in your 2003 white Lexus when you get stuck in traffic. This is usual for you but today it is not so good because you are running late and you were already feeling anxiety when you woke up this morning. You were thinking about certain people at work, and it gave you anxiety. Don't worry, happens to me, too. You are running late also because you had to drop the kids off at school, and the morning traffic over there was no charm cake walk either.

Now, as you are stuck in traffic on a five-lane major highway, I know, I never understood that eight (how can so many lanes be locked!?) you start sucking down your coffee like it is liquid crack to try to calm those nerves. Yeah, sure, that will get those nerves straighten right out.

So now, as you are stuck in dead-stop traffic, the worst of the worst feeling, especially when you are late, anxiety starts getting worse and it starts pumping through you veins harder because you can't move your car at all and it is bothering you.

Next your mind starts to go haywire (crazy) from the anxiety, so you quickly look in your purse for your anxiety meds and realize you forgot them at home! Wonderful, now your anxiety really kicks in and you already start to think crazy things and panic when you don't have your meds and you say to yourself, "Good Lord, I really hope I don't have a panic attack and faint!"

You think about turning your car around so you can go home and grab your meds but you can't because of traffic of course, and plus you are already late. Now your anxiety has just turned into major fear. Right away you eye starts to twitch because you are so nervous and you start already start to have a mild panic attack. Man that was quick! You anxiety works fast, just like mine does.

Quickly behind that, your mild panic attack starts trigger your brain, and then it runs fear through your mind and once it does that, you start saying crazy things to yourself in your head like "I can't be late for work again, I will lose my job," "My boss is going to yell at me," "I can't get fired, I got a family to support!" "Oh, my God, I got to hurry up!"

Now, your anxiety and fear combined makes you get irritant and frustrated because of the situation that is at hand, which really was no different a few minutes ago, but the emotions that are powering you are making it feel different.

You try to move your car through traffic now but it is moving slowly that now you get irritated. You start to fidget with things in your car to try to calm yourself. Traffic starts to break up a little and you try to move your way slowly through traffic, hitting the gas and breaks every two seconds.

Now you are so mad, and you have so much anxiety, fear, and frustration running through your veins, and thoughts running through your head, that you start huffing and puffing, and then practically hyperventilating. You know you are panicking and you want to calm down, so you do something, you call your husband. You think maybe talking to some will help you relax. The phone rings, your husband picks up the phone and then immediately asks, "Why did you call?" and then says, "You know that I am really busy really early in the morning!" and this innocent call turns into a full-out verbal argument! You were hurt by his insensitivity to your emotions, and he also told you to clean the house when you get home! Inconsiderate jerk, I would divorce him, too, if I were you.

Now your frustration has turned into some major anger. You sit in your car in a state of anger and you pray for a way out, and just as you do, the situation takes a turn for the worst as the guy sitting behind you in traffic starts beeping the horn at you even though you are all in dead-stop traffic and there is now where to go. That was a bad time for the person behind you to do that, because now makes your anger turn to into complete RAGE and it takes over your body and you become like you are a possessed demon. The metamorphosis has begun, and horns have now protruded from your head and you are flipping out in your car with all these crazy thoughts running through your mind like "I hate my boss, let him do the work!" "I hate my husband, let him clean the house, that F****** jerk!" and "I HATE MY LIFE! ARRGG! I can't take it anymore! AAAHHE!" And then you start screaming like a lion and punching your steering wheel physically.

You are about ready to explode inside of your car when all of a sudden traffic opens up and starts moving in front of you, thank God, and as soon as you see it move you hit that gas pedal like Richard Petty at Daytona 500, and then start flying down the road doing 100 miles per hour in a twenty-five zone in a fit of Road Rage. You start yelling at people, cutting them off, and curse them off even worse than Andrew Dice Clay would have! You have turned into a complete beast.

Next, you come up to your drive way where you work and pull in so fast that your Lexus goes through the air like something out of a *Dukes of Hazzard* episode! You come crashing into the parking lot like and animal, and pedestrians who are outside walking look at you like you are crazy. You slam your car in park nearly breaking the shifter and then get out of your car, and smoke is coming out from under the hood in mass amounts because you over heated the engine.

Why did all this happen? ALL because all of what was going on in your head, which then triggered your anxiety which then turned into a full on emotional frenzy!

You let what happen to you this morning escalate into what is called or known as the snowball effect. You let that snowball of emotions roll downhill and get bigger. You should have realized how you felling early on, and then tried to stop it early on. Yes, even without your meds. Medication does help my friends, I know this, but I want you to be able to acknowledge those bad emotions early on, and I want you to learn some new techniques so you can stop them from progressing or escalating into something more, and if you read more of this book you can learn just how to do that.

You have to realize what is going with your emotions early before it escalates. That is the best way to learn how to be in control of yourself. It will be a hundred times harder for you to try to calm yourself down once you have already reached the point of anger or rage! It is like trying to tame a wild animal; it is very difficult, if even possible at all. The only way to do it is shoot it with many, many tranquilizers! And remember, the wolf does not perform in a circus. It is just too wild.

So, what is the bottom line? For all the situations that you have ever been in, in your entire life, and ever will be in for the rest of your life, on or off the road, it always comes down to what that situation is making you feel, and how you respond with those feeling?! I wise man named Tony Robbins once said, "Emotions equals two things, Energy plus Motion." It is the energy that we feel, such as Rage, that makes us act out in that aggressive Motion. Hence, the reason why we swing our fist at people or yell at them.

In the very next chapter I have complied many lessons that can help you deal the Rage part of the Road Rage specifically, and in some ways help you notice or stop yourself from letting those emotions ever get to that point to where we don't want them to go: RAGE!

Chapter 4

How Do I Cure My Road Rage?

Well, there is a main solution that I have always thought would be a cure for Road Rage, only problem is, I still have not been able hit the jackpot so I can give it a try. The main cure for Road Rage would to become rich and hire a driver! Although, I will say, if I know you as good as I know myself, even if someone else was driving you around you would probably still roll down the window and yell at someone from the back of your limo if you see someone driving like an idiot.

The next best solution for curing or stopping Road Rage would be to never let your emotions get to the point of Rage! You have to take your emotional freight train of anxiety, frustration, and anger and stop it dead in its tracks before it turns into full on Road Rage and it takes over your body. Once you are in complete Road Rage mode there is no telling what could happen! You got to catch it early and stop it before it gets to that point. You have to notice your emotions early and they will be way easier to control. If not, once you get to into full Road Rage mode the only way to stop you will be to do what they do to wild animals, hit them with a tranquilizer gun and put them to sleep and throw them back in the woods, or in your case, back in jail. Yes, you are like a wild animal when you Road Rage.

But, there is hope, and there are a number of tactics, remedies, therapies, doctors, anger management classes, stress balls, and suggestions that I have used and tried myself over the years that have helped me control my Road Rage, or should I say, stopped it from getting to that point. Yes, most of them have worked many times, not just once, and have helped me I must say and I am happy about that. These have all helped me and kept me from Road Raging many, many times.

So I have compiled a nice-sized list tactics that have helped keep me from Road Raging over the years. I hope you can read and learn some ways that can also help and work for you. So read on and enjoy my fellow Road Ragers and I hope find a cure, a solution, a maybe even some temporary relief from your Road Rage problem.

Don't Bring Anger into Your Car with You

That is one of the biggest things when it comes to Road Rage that a lot of people don't even think about. If you already go to get into your car and you are angry and you leave to go drive somewhere, you have a 95-percent more likely chance of Road Raging than if you got into your car calm.

If you are already upset and you go out driving, you will stand no chance of keeping cool if someone goes to slow in front of you, beeps at you, or God forbid, cuts in front of you. You will fly into a fit of Road Rage instantly and you will then start yelling obscene things at them like "What in the fiery hell are you beeping at, you A** H***!" and "Cut me off that like again and I will run you off the road, J*** O*F!" Oh, and did I mention that while you are yelling at the person to all high hell, you will also try to blind the person you are Road Raging at physically with a brigade of jolting hand gesture that they have never seen before?!

If you want to avoid a major chance at Road Raging, make sure you DO NOT get into your car if you are already angry. You already have the rage going, and now you are on the road. Put two and two together, smarty pants.

Walk It Off

People tell you to go and *walk it off* when you are mad, and not go and *drive it off* for a very specific reason, because we all know the outcome if you do go out driving around when you are upset and mad. It will only result badly.

If you go out walking around when you are upset, you will relieve stress just by moving your muscles around. It is so much safer for someone to go out walking around when they are upset then to go out driving.

If someone upsets you at work, at home, at your parents' house (parents always piss me off), at your friend's house, or at your local bar, don't get into your car right after, dumb ass; go out and walk it off for a while first.

Or if you are already in your car and are driving somewhere and someone on the road upsets you, pull the hell over! I am serious, stop at a rest stop and get out and stretch and walk for a few minutes. Especially when we are driving on long trips we need to get out of the car, unwind a little bit, and walk off and relive some of the tension that built up in the body along the trip. Being confined to a tight space for too long time, like in our car, only makes matters a hundred times worse when we are upset already and tension has built within the body. It is like being trapped like a rat. You are upset and you have nowhere to go. Go run on the hamster wheel for a while. It will cool you down, trust me.

So pull over if you feel like you are going to get into a fit of Road Rage and walk it off for a few minutes. The outcome will be much better than if you decided to stay in your car angry and keep on driving.

Let Someone Else Drive

I wish this was in relation to what I said earlier and becoming rich and just hiring a chauffeur to drive you around all the time, but I am sorry, it is not.

If you have to go out and you are in a bad mood, let someone else drive! Make one of your parents or your significant other drive you. Hey, you might be angry in the car, but at least it won't be you behind the wheel and that is very important for a Road Rager like yourself. You do not want to be behind the wheel mad.

It might save you from getting a ticket, or better yet, getting into another Road Rage altercation and crashing your car! We all know what you are capable of doing when you are driving around in a bad mood.

Also, if you start out on a trip cool, and you have a long drive ahead of you, and somewhere along the line you start to get mad because one to many jerks have already cut you off for the day and you can't take it anymore, and you have other passengers in the car with you, use them. Make them drive so you can cool down for a while. Why should you always be the driver, you should get to relax, too, no!? Or are you like me, you friend always make you drive into New York when you go out clubbing and to The Village because your friends are punks and they are too scared to drive in the city, so you always end up doing it.

Example Story: Picture it, you are a tall, well-built, twenty-two-year-old white meathead, and you just got into one of those head-twisting arguments with your girlfriend and she has got you all fired up (really mad), and she decided to start this argument right before the two of you are about to walk out the door to go to dinner. Nice job, honey. You know what, now let her drive! Even though she is mad also from the argument, we know she won't Road Rage like you will. Women just don't do Road Rage as much as men do.

But, if by some chance your girlfriend is of those crazy Road Rage women, like my ex, that also likes to throw things and yell at people on the road when she is in a bad mood, then you should both pitch in and take a cab! Don't feel embarrassed; we have all had a crazy ex-girlfriend that used to Road Rage like that.

Make Your Car Like Home

If you want to keep your Road Rage from acting up, make your car like home. Make your car comfortable. When you are in your comfort zone, like at home in your nice cozy space in the bedroom, where it smells nice and everything is clean, you don't seem to get angry, do you? In fact, you get rather relaxed when you go to this cozy place. Make your car similar to this!

Make you can smell nice, decorate it a little bit (put up a picture on the dashboard), buy a seat cover, buy a steering wheel cover, make it unique, and make it comfortable. When you feel comfortable in your car like you do at home, you are way less likely to get into an angry mood. Just feeling uncomfortable puts a chip on everyone's shoulder, everyone knows that!

For instance, even if you drive a plumbing van for work like I used to that smells like S*** all the time, literally, clean it the hell up and make it nice! I would clean my truck at least once a week and carry Febreze (that nice-smelling spray that is made for everything) in the van to spay it down with all the time. That nice, sweet smell of Febreze rather than feces used to keep me relaxed.

Who the hell wants to drive around all day in a vehicle that they can't even breathe in? Not me, that is for sure. When the van smelt horrible (especially on hot days) I would speed from place to place Road Raging and practically pushing people out of my way and off the road just so I could get the hell out of that van and catch my breath.

Grab Your Stress Ball

Are you too stressed out and about ready to flip out and go into a fit of Road Rage! If you are, grab that stress ball and calm the heck down. There is nothing else more relaxing then grabbing and squeezing that sand filled balloon and pretending that you are choking the neck of the person that just made you mad, like the person who just tried to run you off of the road and gave you the finger, rather than actually doing so and going to jail.

Whether it be someone who made you mad before you ever even got into your car or someone who made you mad on the road, use the stress ball! It is such a wonderful feeling visualize yourself choking someone. Just don't get too caught up in the moment of pretending and forget that you are driving. Happened to me once, and I almost crashed.

Also, it is the movement of the muscles that helps to keep you calm and helps relieve tension. We are always so crammed in our little compact cars that we can barely move a muscle and we feel trapped, which basically, we are trapped. Especially when we are stuck in traffic on the highway. You can't just park your car on the side of the road and get out, like in town.

Moving those muscles will help the brain to relieve that trapped feeling and calm those nerves of yours and help to keep you from going into Road Rage mode.

To buy an actual stress ball I think you can buy them online, or you can go get a similar item, a hand strengthener that they usually sell at your local sports store.

They sell sand filled bags that are made to build muscle, same exact thing as a stress ball, or they have metal ones that you have to squeeze together with all of you might. Football players and other sports people use them to strengthen their hand muscles so they can catch a ball easier.

There you go, so now you can calm down and build muscle. Like they say, killing two birds with one stone buddy. In a last precaution, if you really need a stress ball and can't fine one, use an old hacky sack (those beanbag balls that stoners kick around).

Loosen Your Death Grip

Next time you are driving and you start to get angry and feel like you are going to go into a fit of Road Rage and start yelling at people and cutting them off, take a notice to this! Take a noticed to how tight your hands are grabbing your steering wheel Bruce Lee when you are angry and tense!

When people are relaxed and are cruising around you can always see them in this posture that is known to us in the streets as a *Gangster Lean*.

A Gangster Lean is when the driver of a vehicle lays and sits so far back that you can barely see them driving at all, and they have one arm kind of hanging over the steering wheel all nice and lose and comfortable like. They are driving around Gangster Style (taking it easy). And if you must know, people who drive with a Gangster Lean usually drive really big and really nice cars, like a 1979 Lincoln Mark V, and they are usually driving really, really, slow.

But when you see people who are driving around in traffic that are in a rush or are agitated you can see the posture that they are using. It is known in the street and called a *Stick Up Their A*** posture.

They drive with their seat all the way against the dashboard, their back is straight as a board and not bent at all, and they have their hands two hands wrapped around the steering so tightly that they look like they are going to pull the damn thing off and hit themselves in the face with it.

You will notice that as your emotions change, so does your driving position and posture. When you are as mad as a mad dog next time you are driving and you are about to go into Road Rage mode take notice to this. Notice to how tight you have got your hands on that steering wheel. If we took off your steering wheel and gave you a brick to grab you would probably crush it into pieces. That is how tight your grip is when you are mad, you just don't realize it.

So if you want to keep that Road Rage from escalating, loosen up that grip a little bit next time. You will notice that when you do it will relieve muscle tension all the way from your hands, through your arms, and all the way into parts of your back in neck. It may sound crazy but as soon as your muscles begin to relax a few seconds after loosening your grip you will begin to feel the difference in your body almost immediately!

So best bet, next time you are about to Road Rage, do what you do when you drive around on your day off and are relaxed. Roll down the window, put your left arm out the window, drive with your right hand loosely on the steering wheel, throw the seat back a click, and relax, pal!

Road Rage Buddha says, if you can change your physical posture from angry to calm, your mind will soon follow.

Manage Your Time

You have to learn to manage your time, sleepyhead. I know it, and you know it, that more than half the time we even get mad on the road and get into a Road Rage altercation is because we are running late for something and feel like we are being pressured.

And not too many people at all can handle pressure, especially when they are in their cars! Once we are pressured we all know what comes next, we start to get anxiety, and what do we do when we get anxiety? We tell ourselves crazy things in our heads that are not true like, if we are not at this certain location at this certain time then something drastic might happen! Like, if I don't get to work on time I might lose my job, or if I don't get to the school in time they might throw my kids outside and some stranger might steal them! It is always the worst-case scenario and things that are not true, of course. Why would we think positive, right!?

This always happens to us when we are running late and we begin to think horrible thoughts like that. Once we do that then the pressure builds up within our heads and then we begin to panic. Right after panic is Road Rage! And it is all because of the time baby. If you had more time these thing would not happen.

Example Story: Picture it, you are a forty-eight-year-old white male who works as a cook at a restaurant, and this morning, you hit the snooze button three extra times because you took to many Klonopin (anxiety medication) last night so you had a hard time waking up because of it, so you ended up getting up a half-hour late for work this morning. Oh, boy, here we go.

You stumble out of bed in a hurry hitting and knocking a few things over and rushing to get ready. You get ready in five minutes, rush out the door, and then jump into your car which is a 1979 Chevy Nova and you take off in it like it is the Batmobile leaving from the Bat Cave. You take off down the road with flames coming out of your tail pipes and head onto the highway toward work. As soon as you pull up the ramp onto the highway, boom, you hit dead-stop traffic. What, did you forget you left thirty minutes late? There is always traffic at 8:30 because 90 percent of people are just like you, always behind and don't know how to manage their time, either.

So now you inch your way through traffic in your Batmobile for the next half-hour behind this same damn car. You start to feel the pressure about being late and you because of it you start tell yourself crazy things in your head once again, like "Oh, man, that new guy at work is going to look better than me now!" "They are all probably there laughing about me at work," and "The boss is probably waiting by the door for me with a whip!" Now you are panicking and you feel the Road Rage start to come on.

After being stuck in traffic for another minute you can finally see your exit for work up ahead! But there is one problem, that one damn car that you have been stuck behind the whole time while driving in traffic, who breaks lights are permanently imbedded in your brain for the rest of the day, will not move up the extra inch so you can get over into the passing lane.

Here it comes, *beeeeep*, *beeeep*, as you slam down on the horn and keep on hitting it like you are giving it CPR (Cardiopulmonary Resuscitation). You go into full-on Road Rage mode and keep beeping, yelling, and shaking violently in your car until the guy in front of you gets scared and moves their car out of your way!

Now, you are able to get your car by and you take off up the highway ramp like a madman and giving all the cars behind you the finger. You keep your Road Rage going the rest of the way to work beeping at everyone and flying past people who are going to slow and cursing at them for doing so. You yell, "Get the F*** out of my way, slowpoke, I got to get to work! They are laughing and making a mockery of me over there!"

You know what Road Rage Buddha has to say about this one, don't you? Road Rage is just a side-effect of running late!

If you had more time none of that ever would have happened to you and you never would have Road Raged like that. It is all from running late and the pressure was on that made you do that.

When you run late and are strapped for time all this is more likely to happen to you.

You will feel pressured when in you are driving.

You have more of a chance of getting caught in traffic.

You have more of a chance of becoming upset.

You will most likely drive faster and then there will be more of a chance of a dangerous accident.

You will have more of a chance at getting pulled over and getting a ticket.

You will have more of a chance at getting into a Road Rage altercation because you will probably curse at someone who is driving to slow.

What kind of things can you do to manage your time so you don't have to run into these situations? There are a bunch of solutions for the type of people who are going to be late to their own funeral. Such as...

Stop staying out late and drinking so much.

Set your alarm clock earlier and buy a really loud one. If it is not loud enough keep it on your bed under your pillow. I used to have to do that.

Leave for work earlier so you can avoid traffic. No traffic no pressure.

Set your clock in your car fifteen minutes ahead/fast so you are always a little ahead of yourself. It works. A lot of people do that, as do I.

If you family are the reason why you run late all the time, lie to them. Tell them you have to be wherever that it is that you have to be earlier than you actually have to be.

If you made dinner reservations for 7:00 P.M., tell your family that they are for 6:30 P.M. This way when you show up a half-hour late you will be right in time.

Buy a time machine when they come out. I am sure they will be just as popular as iPhones are now, in the future.

Play Those Tapes

And no, I am not talking about playing those heavy metal music tapes like I used to. Yes, I was that crazy kid in your town who used to drive around blasting Metallica, Slayer, Ozzy, and Pantera tapes in his car like a maniac and banging his head against the steering wheel to the music! Hey, it was fun at the time.

But I have now changed my crazy ways and I no longer do that. I went from a one-track mind, kind of negative, kind of crazy, and kind of out-of-control person, into a full-throttle motivational guru.

And just for the record, I am not saying heavy metal music is bad and I don't listen to it anymore. I just don't act crazy and violent when I listen to it like I used to.

You see, music all depends on the state of the mind of the person who is listening to it and how they relate to the music. I was a crazy, drunken, violent, out-of-control metal head that was listening to Metallica. How else would I take the music besides literally and think that I was a metal warrior from the past? I really believed that I was reincarnated at one point and was brought back. Listening to that music when you are already in a negative or crazy frame of mind, mixed with having a powerful/vivid imagination does nothing but two things. Either it gets your ready to go into the mosh pit (a dance circle where people beat the S*** out of each other) and get ready to thrash dance, or if you are behind the wheel of a car, God forbid, it gets you ready to run people right off of the F****G road, as if you are driving a battering ram and you are ready to take out the gates of a castle.

Now, being that I have changed, for the most part, and I have grown up a bit, and I am a little more positive and motivational and not in that crazy drunken state of mind anymore, I can listen to that heavy metal music and I can relate to the music from an artistic point of view. I can relate emotionally to what the lyrics and song have to say/express, and I can enjoy it, and not actually take it literally and let it go to my head like before.

"Well, what do you listen to now, Mr. Positive," you ask?

Well, for starters, any low and relaxing music is better for you than any fast-paced loud music. Listing to fast-paced loud music is like a soundtrack to a racing movie or something. You have seen movies like *The Fast and the Furious*. When there is a race scene on, listen to the music. The faster the music, the faster you will want to drive. Same concept as the movies is the very same concept for you in real life, trust me on this.

Next, the best thing to listen to that will help you not Road Rage is self-help tapes. And who else's self-help tapes would I recommend beside the man that has helped me change my ways, but none other than Anthony (Tony) Robbins! "Who the hell is that," you ask? You know, that big guy from the movie *Shallow Hal*, with Jack Black.

When you listen to some of Tony Robbins' tapes when you drive around, not only will it keep you calm and positive when you drive, but it will keep you calm and more positive throughout your whole day.

You know you can always use that extra motivation in the morning besides your cup of coffee, your wife complaining, and the morning traffic before you walk into work.

When I would listen to my Tony Robbins tapes on my way to work in the morning, not only did I drive better, but it was like I strived to be better at work every day. It helped out me out a lot. I stopped using the tapes for a few weeks and of course I got pulled over for driving like a maniac one morning, and I got into an argument with one of the people at work.

Listening to self-help/motivational tapes helps us remind ourselves what we are supposed to be doing in life, why we should be doing it, and how we should be doing it. We forget these thing at times when we do the same routine every day for eight years and become like robots and lose all motivation, and fall into that pit of using dry sarcasm (dry drunk attitude) to get by in life. What, you think I don't know you? Another day in paradise, right? My wife has all my money, right? Living the dream, right?

Or, listen to some nice, easy, inspirational music when you drive around like Beethoven.

Also there are many other self-help/motivational people to choose from that have audio CDs/tapes just like Tony Robbins. All you have to do is go to the books on audio section in Barnes & Noble and fine some. You have people like Louise Hay, Michael Bernard Beckwith, and Esther and Jerry Hicks that all have great stuff to listen to. Also another really good one that I have on audio book is *The Secret*. The Secret is a really good one that has helped millions already, and to tell you the truth, it is where I got my start and my main reason for wanting to go back to my childhood dream of becoming a writer.

So playing those tapes will not only help you with you Road Rage people, it will help you in every aspect of your life that you may be having trouble with, so go for it.

Call Someone

If you feel like you are going to go into a fit of Road Rage, call someone. Just don't dial and drive at the same time because we don't want you to get into an accident! And it is illegal to talk on the phone and drive anyhow, unless you put your phone on speaker phone, or have a head set (Bluetooth). Pull over for a few moments if you have to while you call someone. It is much safer.

A good way to calm down if you are driving around alone and are really upset for some reason or another is to call someone. A lot of times when we drive around alone and have no one to talk to we go into a bad place in our heads. It is the only place that we ever get some time to ourselves to think, and then when we think, we think about all the stress that we having going on in our lives. Next thing you know, boom, we are upset and on the road, not a good combination.

And if you do decide to call someone, don't call the person who knows how to upset you more than everyone else and might actually make matters worse for you. Like your boyfriend who never pays attention to you when you call to vent because he is too busy playing video games or hanging out with his so-called boys. If he calls his friends his "boys," honey, then you are dating a boy, sorry to let you know. So calling him will only make you a thousand times more pissed off and you will end up throwing the phone out the window at someone.

Call an old best friend that you have not talked to in a while! They are the best to talk to. You always reminisce and talk and laugh about the good old times, and if they were not that good, you still both know how to look back and laugh about the bad things. That's what real friends are for. So, if you are a man, give your old Army buddy a call and ask him how him and his family are doing these days and go over some old war stories, and if you are a woman, call you mother and tell her how much you hate the boy that you are dating.

Get Out of Your Shell and Hit the Racetrack!

Yes, you heard it right, Mr. Speedy Gonzalez. Since you like to speed so much and be so daring on the regular road when you are angry, why don't you go hit the racetrack to blow off some of that steam?! That is what the professionals do. They drive like human beings on the regular roads and like rabid animals on the racetrack. That is where you're supposed to, and you are allowed to do it, imagine that. The best part about it is, is that you don't have to put any innocent bystanders life's at risk with your crazy Road Rage escapades and speeding when you do it on the racetrack. You may be put your own life on the line a little, but not really because there are so many safety rules and standards that you have to go by so it is almost impossible to get hurt.

If you look it up online I am sure you can find more than one or two racetracks that are no more than an hour away, and that is even if you live right in the middle of New York City. Pennsylvania (Pennsyltucky) that has more than one racetrack is only an hour drive from the The Big City and so is English Town Racetrack. English Town in right in south New Jersey.

You can go down, pay for the day and you can bring almost and street legal car onto one of their straight quarter-mile racetrack. Yes, even if you have a brand-new girly car, the Scion (those funny-looking new cars), and want to bring it to a track and see how fast your girl car can go.

All you really have to do is bring a helmet and a car that is no faster than ten seconds in the quarter-mile. If you are brining your Scion to the track, I am sure you won't have to worry about the ten-second part. Not even if you put a 454 Chevy motor in a Scion would it run ten seconds in a quarter-mile. If you have a car that is faster than ten seconds, then you need to start putting roll cages and other safety equipment on your car and that can get crazy (really) expensive, but if you have a car that is going that fast you just might have the money for it.

Also, there are many dirt bike tracks in Pennsylvania that you can just bring your own dirt bike, or a friend's dirt bike if you don't own one, pay for the day, and ride the day away! All you need to bring is a bike, a helmet, and the proper safety gear to wear. You can go out and tear up the dirt and hit jumps all day long until your B***s falls off.

So get out there and go tear it up, people, the right way! All you need is a few dollars and one weekend day to go down to a local race-track to have some fun. If you don't want to race on the first day, it is always fun to go and watch others race. It is very exciting.

Hitting a real racetrack is a million times better when you want blow off some long-built-up steam rather than trying to do it on the regular streets. It is also a million times safer. There is nothing like it when you are on the racetrack lined up neck and neck with another person and that light turns green and you are allowed to go as fast as you can go all the way to the finish line. It is one hell of a feeling, especially when you win! And you know what, it teaches you what most sports do, and what is called "good sportsmanship!" You beat the hell out of each other, knock each other down, and then you get up, shake hands, and you go your separate ways as a better person. That almost never happens when people Road Rage at each other.

So, go get on out there and get your ass to the racetrack. Go dig up some dirt on a motocross. Go burn some rubber and some gas at the racetrack. I promise it will be 100-percent worth it, and I even bet you will fall in love with it and will be at the racetrack all the time.

Take a Look to the Sky, Just before You Die
- **Metallica** (For Whom the Bell Tolls)

Yes, and I am referring to the verse in the song "For Whom the Bell Tolls" by Metallica. It is a verse that speaks loudly and clearly to a guy like me that believes in out of sight out of mind. What I realized as I got older and worked on my Road Rage problem, along with a ton of other psychological problems that I had at the time, was that the main problem was what I was always focusing on at the moment. It is very simple to explain.

If I am mad at you, and I keep on looking at you, I will just continue to keep on getting more and more mad at you. If I turn and walk away, leave the situation alone for a while and I don't see you, hence, out of sight out of mind, I will start to calm down. Same theory goes for people on that road that are upsetting me.

Example Story: Picture it. You are a twenty-eight-year-old white male who is driving in a 2001 black Cadillac, and you are driving home from your sister's house. And as you are driving, you see a horrible driver on the road. This person driving on the road in front of you is all over the place. Back and forth, left to right, up and down, and weaving in and out of traffic.

You noticed them when you both went to make a right turn at an intersection about a mile back, and you saw them curb check (hop the curb with their rear tires) the sidewalk and almost flip their car.

As you drive along behind the horrible driver your start to get upset because not only are they driving like crap, but they are also driving way too slow and they don't seem to know where in the hello they are even going! Now, you look at the person driving and with your laser eyes, and you notice that they seem to be reading a piece of paper, so right away you think, this person is reading directions, and you are ab-solutely right because as you look, you see the driver looking at street signs, and not at the road.

Now, you get mad and you make a wish in your head. Your wish is this: "I wish this person would move the hell out my way so I can pass already!" I think your wish just came true.

The horribly lost driver puts on their right blinker as if they are going to make a right turn. So you notice that he puts on his blinker and just as he slows down to go and make the turn you start to go around them. In you mission to get around them quickly, you kind of go over the double yellow lines, which is illegal, but screw 'em at this point, you want to get around this guy.

As you go over to pass the horrible driver takes off their blinker and decided to floor it. The horrible driver keeps on going straight now and puts you in a situation where you get stuck on wrong side of the road and is trying to make you get into a head-on collision with another car! You jam on your breaks and swerve back behind the horrible lost driver and you nearly escape death. Well, we already know what is going on through your mind by this point. Wait until no cars are com-ing and I am going to cut him off and run him off of the road. You are also thinking about ramming your car right into the back of him and pushing him of the road now, but you won't do that because then you would be at fault! The other choice that is running through your head now might just follow him to his destination and when he gets out of his car run up and strangle him. Hey, this all seems kind of crazy, but the guy almost did just kill you.

So, anyone would be mad that is in your situation and be thinking the same exact things that you are, sure, but is it right, NO, not at all. That is the complete wrong way to think and act, and as long as you stay behind this person you will continue to keep on thinking those things, and might actually act them out! I know I have.

The best solution to this situation would to be turn off and forget about the guy! Pull over and let him keep on going to the point where you don't see him anymore. Make a turn onto a side road. Make a F****** illegal U-turn for all I care. Do whatever it is that you have to do as to not see the horribly lost driver anymore.

As soon as you don't see the horrible driver anymore you will start to calm down automatically, trust me. Yes, he may be in your mind for weeks, and yes, you may have even written down his license plate and plan on paying him visit one day in the future for what he did to you, but as long as you don't see that horrible driver anymore you will eventually be fine and like they say, the situation will cool itself down. Remember, out of sight out of mind.

The problem with most people is our focus and what we do with it. Whatever we focus on gets bigger, whether it is good or bad. If we keep on focusing on happiness and good, it will only get bigger. If we keep on focusing on anger and bad things, it will only get bigger.

One thing I do when I am driving and the road and I start focusing on someone that does not know how to drive and begins to piss me the hell off, I take a look to the sky! No, I do not mean I take my eyes off the road and start to go into meditation while I am driving. I just kind of look at the skyline right above the cars. I try not to look at the car directly anymore that is upsetting me.

I mean, take a look at the clouds or the skyline as you drive down the highway for a change and take notice to how beautiful it is instead of focusing on every negative thing on the road. I know it is a tough thing to do at first, but is very relaxing looking at the sky and you will forget about whoever is on the road in front of you that is pissing you off, I swear. It is so freeing to look and to think that just a few feet above you on the road in the sky there is no such thing as traffic.

So next time you are driving down the road and you are in a bad mood, take a look to the sky, just before you die, it could be the last time you will.

Turn That "M" in "Me" Upside Down and Make It a "WE"
If you are a true Road Rager and tend to feel insulted on the road when people upset you, then I am sure you say things to yourself in your head like this.

- The way this person in front is driving is making *me* angry.
- Why did he pull out in front of *me* like that?
- This person is driving way to slow for *me*.
- This guy is holding *me* up, and *I* am going to be late now.
- If that guy's car come near *me* there is going to be a problem.
- How come these kids want *me* to pick them up from school?
- Why is it always *me, me, me*!?

Wow, those are some selfish thoughts that you have going in in your head their pal. What, were you an only child? I am sorry, I know that was a low blow, but good luck living with anybody happily with that mentality.

You have to remember something, pal, life ain't all about you/me. It never was and it never will be. Life is about helping others and not being selfish. It is about who we can help, and not who can help us.

And the only way to get rid of that selfish attitude that you have, and make it anywhere on the road of life safely and not just the road to work is this. You have to turn that "M" in *me* upside down and make it a "W," a *we* thing.

You know that *we* are all on the road together. What you have to do is stop being so selfish and sometimes think about the other people for a change. What you should be saying in your head is...

- Why are *we* all stuck in traffic this morning?
- Why do *we* all have to pay such high toll fairs and taxes?
- If there was no roadwork and construction *we* would not have any traffic today.
- If they open that closed off lane *we* will all be able to pass.

And if you can't take the *ME* out of your head, and you want to keep using it in an unselfish manner, then maybe you can say and do things like...

- Let *me* move out of this guy's way, maybe *he* is in a rush.
- Let *me* not beep at this guy who is in front of me, maybe *he* is having a bad day as it is.
- Let *me* stop and help this guy out with the flat tire.

Like I said, life is all about what we can do for others. Being selfish gets you nowhere but lonely and empty. The more selfish we are in life, the less we have. The more giving and helping we become, the more we get back.

Next time you are on the road and you feel like Road Raging, stop, and make a simple gesture as to go out of your way to let someone pass and let some go in front of you. The outcome is always better rather than if you try to block people and cut them off. Sometimes, and only some of the times, people even compensate you for your kindness and you even get wave and a smile back rather than a finger and a pissed of look. Isn't that something!?

Last, but Not Least, Pray

Praise to the powers that be. I do believe in a higher power, a God, and a creator of the everything as we know it, even though I do not belong to any specific religion. I like to think of myself as spiritual and believe that my God is The Spirit of the Universe itself, you know, kind of like *The Force* that they talk about from *Star Wars*. No one can tell me that does not exist, not even myself, so that is what I like to believe in and pray, too.

If you do not believe in anything, then believe in yourself and pray to that. You do exist and no one, not even yourself, can ever tell you any different.

And there is more power in believing in yourself then you can ever even imagine. If fact, that is what they say that the Holy Spirit is itself. A love and a belief in yourself. When you believe in yourself the possibilities are endless.

If you are a patriotic person like I am also, pray to the forefathers who made this country that believed in something greater than themselves that made this beautiful land that we call America so that we may live in it as free men.

I salute flags whenever I pass one as I am driving and pray and am grateful for all the people who have gave their lives for this wonderful country and for the freedom that I am allowed to have in it. That is a real thing to pray to, and no one can ever take that from you as long as America stands as One Nation under God.

Why pray, do you say? I will let Road Rage Buddha answers this one. Road Rage Buddha says, prayer is a last resort for most, but a first for some.

There is a lot of power in prayer. A lot of people just don't realize it until they are at their end of their ropes in life and feel like they have no were else to turn, and then they pray. There is no other feeling like hitting rock bottom and having nowhere else to go, then praying, and having your prayers answered and having miraculous things happen to you. There are no words to describe what it is like when you pray and wonderful things happen to you.

Most people are very connected to what is called a foxhole prayer. It is when you are stuck in a hole and you pray that the dogs don't get your ass because you got nowhere else to run, and you say things like "If this cop don't give me a ticket, God, I swear I will never speed again!" These are common forms of prayer and I am sure you are familiar with them.

But I am not talking about BULLS*** praying, I am talking about real praying. People pray hard when it comes to situations like this.

The guy who has been taking the bus for the last five years and is sitting at the bus stop is praying that he will get a car when he can save the money to do so. I am talking about the guy who lost his job because his car broke down and he can't afford a new one and is praying that he can come up with enough money to buy some food for his kids tonight. I am talking about the kids who live in another country and has never even sat in a car because they live in poverty and pray that they may one day even drive in a car, never mind own one.

So what I am saying is not to pray to relieve us from Road Rage, or to get us out of tickets, but to pray for thankfulness that we even have a car! Forty percent of the world does not even drive so how does that make you feel about your car now. We should be grateful to live in a land that cars and roads are even so accessible so that we may do as we please, but yet, we still get angry at each other and we Road Rage just because we have to sit in a little bit of traffic some times.

Get over it, think about it, and be grateful that you even have a car. The only time I was ever grateful in the past that I even had a car was when I lost my license and could not drive it. I was grateful when I got back in it, and then within a few weeks I went back to my old ways. Being pissed off that other people are even allowed on the road with me, being mad that I had a crappy car, and Road Raging at people when they pissed me off. It happened many times. I just always returned to that metal state of ungratefulness.

So I try to pray often now as to help me be in what is called an attitude of gratitude. When I am grateful I always seem to be in a happier place, and that good place to be in when you are behind the wheel of a car and stuck in traffic.

So like they say, don't pray for patience because God will put you in a situation where you need to be patient, like stuck in traffic. If you want to pray, say a prayer in gratitude and thankfulness!

I pay and I am thankful for the roads that America has made so beautifully so that I may travel to work on them in safe manner.

I pray and I am thankful that I have a wonderful job so that I can afford my wonderful car so that I may drive in it wherever I damn well please.

I pray and I am thankful for the wonderful life my car has provided for me.

I pray and I am thankful for all the wonderful roads and trucks that travel along with me so that they can bring food to the supermarket so that I may eat.

I pray and I am thankful that America has given me opportunity to be a free person and to the people who gave their lives so that I may do so.

I pray and I am thankful that my selfish A* * even has a car.

So pray away, my good friends, and get yourself to a better place.

The words we speak have true power, and the greater/positive the words, the greater our lives shall be.

Chapter 5

What Do I Do if I Run into a Road Rager?

Even though you are reading this book, and you may have even gotten a high-point score on the Road Rage test and think that you are a bad-ass Road Rager and no one will ever mess with you on the road, think again. I will only say this and warn you once so listen closely. There is, and there will always be someone out there that is crazier than you are, trust me on this.

You have to remember, there are people out there who have been locked away for the rest of their lives because of how crazy they are, and you may never meet them, or you might? What if they decide to break out the nut house one day, steal a car, drive around, and the run into you on the road and give you a hard time. What, you don't think it is possible? Imagine getting into a Road Rage altercation on the road with a real nutcase. How do you think that picture would turn out!? Just as you imagined, them jumping on your hood naked and then trying to kill you.

Or, you may also have a situation similar to mine, where you used to be the crazy person on the road doing the Road Raging and chasing people down when you were younger. Now you are way too old to be doing stuff like that and you are trying to better yourself with your smarter and more responsible ways.

Too bad yesterday, though, you went out for a ride and had some Young Punk started yelling at you on the road and calling you profanities all because you were driving too slow. They were doing to you the very same thing to you did to a million people in the past when you were younger. Karma is a big, fat, nasty, old B****, my friend.

So whatever the case may be, whatever we did in the past, and however crazy we think currently are or we used to be, we should not Road Rage in the anymore because we could bump into the wrong person and it could end badly for us. We should avoid it at all costs, even if that means having to avoid someone who is already Road Raging at you! Like I said in the last part, let it go,

Yes, I am sorry to say it, but like they say, "It takes more of a man to walk away from a fight," or in this case, "It takes more of a man to drive away from a Road Rage altercation!" and it is so true. You don't believe or care for much when you are younger, but when you are older and you have a lot to lose, you have to swallow your pride and walk, or drive away from a fight.

So there are a few suggestions and tricks that I know work when it comes to keeping a Road Rager away from you when they are on a war path and doing dangerous things, like trying to chase you down, yelling at you, and throwing things at you. "How do you know they work," you ask? I know they work because these are the things people used on me when I was doing the Road Raging! That is how I know, real-life experience. People have used these tricks on me and they worked. And luckily, I have only had to use these myself once because I actually ran into a person that was crazier than me on the road, and I feared for my life. Just like I said, I always thought I was the craziest person on the road doing the Road Rage, but it turned out not to be true when I ran into a guy that jumped on the back of my car and smashed in my back window in a fit of Road Rage.

So here are a few tips and tricks that you can use to so you can avoid getting into a Road Rage altercation with even the most dangerous of Road Ragers.

Never Look Them in the Eyes!

One way to completely avoid a Road Rage altercation altogether when someone is driving right next to you on the road and yelling profanities at you, would be to not look at them. One thing I stated earlier, out of sight, out of mind. If someone is beside you and they are yelling at you, and even though you know that they are doing this, do yourself the favor and don't even bother to turn your head and look at them, because as soon as you do, and you look at them in the eyes, it will only escalate from there, trust me on this. Mister Miyagi from *Karate Kid* always said, "Daniel Son, always look your opponent in the eye!" but I say in this case, take the latter route. Road Rage Buddha says, "Never look your Road Rage opponent in the eye!"

You see, whenever people used to make me mad on the road, cut me off, go slow in front of me, not drive how I think they were supposed to be driving, and I would go into Road Rage mode, my first move, would always be to try to pull up right next to the person who was driving that pissing me off, as they were driving, I would begin to yell at them personally and tell them how I felt. It was my way of venting and getting their attention, and it just made me feel better.

If the person I was yelling at did not even turn to look at me, never mind yell back at me, I would instantly back away because I would say to myself, "That's right, they don't want none of this!" And what I mean by that is, they don't want to argue with me because they are afraid of me, and you want the Road Rager to think that.

If you don't look the Road Rager in the eyes he will think you are scared and he will back away. Road Ragers go around trying to pump fear into people so that they will move out of their way on the road, and if you look at them in the eye, you are engaging and you are NOT showing fear, and they will then try harder to try to scare you. Do not engage! Let them go, don't look at them, and they will eventually leave you alone because they will get frustrated that you are not giving them any attention.

Paying no mind to the Road Rager is the best way to stop an altercation from happening completely if you ask me.

I know it is a tough situation to ignore when you have someone yelling profanity at you and giving you the finger as you are driving along and trying to mind your own business, but you have to forget about them and they will go away.

And if they don't leave you alone and they continue to persist you into getting into a more serious Road Rage altercation with them, I have more suggestions for you to try ahead in this chapter that will help you get out of that. But just let me tell you, if you do turn to look at the Road Rager and you give them the attention that they are looking for, and your start yelling back, it will only escalate right from their and it will only end badly. Once again, do not engage.

In karate class, there are people to stop the fighting and break it up when things get ugly, but on the road, there is not, so don't take Mister Miyagi advice in this case, please.

Do Not Try to Outrun Them!

If you are driving down the road, and you cut someone off by accident, and it just happens to be some crazy person that is having a bad day, and they begin to start chasing you down the road in their car as you ae driving and you can see that this person is clearly Road Raging at you, whatever you do, do NOT try to outrun them. Trying to outrun someone is one of the worst and most dangerous things you can possibly do if you are in the middle of a Road Rage altercation. Speeding when in a heated situation not only puts your own life in danger, but everyone else's.

There are a few reasons why you should not try to outrun a Road Rager.

Number one, if they see you running they will automatically think that you are afraid and then they will be enticed to chase you more. That is what Road Ragers do, they feed on fear. They can smell/see it. Road Ragers are like bees, bears, and lions!

Number two, if you take off like a bat out of hell, they might also think that you are trying to race with them if you start to drive faster, and if there is one thing a Road Rager loves to do beside yell at people on the road and curse them out, it is race with them, especially in heated situations.

If you do decide to speed up, which you should not, but if you do because you are nervous and you don't want to be near the Road Rager because they are making you afraid, and they still continue to follow you and try to race with you, there is another option when things come to this point, but this is a dangerous and risky one, so please do not try it unless it comes to this point. Once you speed up and they start to chase you, let them try to race with you, and as soon as they pull up alongside of you so that can yell at you again, jam on your breaks and let them pass you so you can then make an emergency escape! Once they pass you, take the next exit or turn off right away, even if it is not your exit, and they will keep on going. This is called the old, "Slip and Dip" technique. Only use this method like a said if you are in a really heated situation because it can be dangerous.

If they are ahead of you on the road and you turn off to get away from them, there is almost no way that a Road Rager will reverse to go back up a highway the wrong way, or street and cause a major accident just to chase you down, no matter how much you pissed them off on the road. They will think you are a punk and just keep on going, and hey, if it works and you get out of there safely who cares what anyone thinks. All that matters is that you get out of there safe.

I do have to throw this in there, though. If by some chance the Road Rager does go in reverse, and they go backward up a highway to start chasing you again after you just pulled a fast one on them like that, and they start chasing you down again, I will tell you two things.

Number one, you are dealing with a dangerous person. "How dangerous," you ask!? Maybe as dangerous as The New Joker from the movie *The Dark Night*.

Number two, this is more than a Road Rage altercation, and the person who is chasing you is doing so because either you owe them a ton of money, or you had sex with their mother!

So you better think really quickly where you can get some money, or you need to remember who you need to make an amends to and call them up quick.

So all in all, the best thing to do if you have a Road Rager following you and trying to chase you, is slow down and drive as normal as possible. That is it. They will eventually get frustrated by your normal driving and they will have to leave you alone.

That what the Road Rager's whole main purpose was, to make you scared and run, and now it isn't happening! How do you think they feel now knowing that you are not scared not matter how close they get to your bumper, and however many times they beep at you and give you the finger? You have to just be cool (remain calm) and stick to your guns (keep mentally strong) and drive as normal as possible. Eventually the Road Raging jerk will go away.

Do Not Retaliate

The last thing you want to do to a Road Rager is retaliate, because that is the first thing that will not only make you look as bad as the person Road Raging at you, but it will also give you the same amount of tickets and violations that the Road Ragers is going to get if the cops show up!

Example Story: Picture it, you are a forty-year-old, bald, fat, white dude who is driving down the road in his 2006 Toyota Camry and coming home from a dentist appointment and minding your own business one day, when all of a sudden, as you are driving along, you look in your rearview mirror and you notice some Road Rager going crazy behind you.

There they are, the Road Raging Road Rager, beeping the horn and yelling at you with all of their might! The Road Rager is beeping their horn at you so intensely that for a moment, you actually thought a firetruck was behind you and that is why you looked.

Now, as you look in your side view, you see this Road Raging lunatic come around you and now they are trying to pass you on the wrong side of the road, literally going head on into oncoming traffic, and you don't even know why this person is acting this way or what the hell is going on!

Next thing you know, as this crazy Road Raging dude decides to pass you on the wrong side of the road, as he does he get right alongside of you he stick his whole arm out of the window and he throw his Starbucks coffee all over your car! You gasp and you see a cup flying through the air and then this crazy persons coffee hits your windshield, and it explodes into a blinding vison of Double Mocha Frappuccino.

Right away you panic because you can't see anything, so you immediately hit the windshield washer fluid button right away to clean the coffee off of your windshield so you don't get into an accident.

Now, as you can see again, you see the Road Rager cut in front of you because you were forced to slow down, and now you go from being a cool and calm human individual, to then turning bright green and becoming full of muscle and adrenaline, and as you do, you then start to pound on your steering wheel in a fit of fury, nearly breaking it, and then you scream out, "How dare the son of a B**** do that to me!" Next thing you know you turn around, reach onto the floor behind your seat, grab an empty glass iced tea bottle, and then you decide to do the same thing in return, retaliate! Bad idea, pal. Now, you hit the gas pedal as hard as possible because you are so mad and your car nearly takes flight. Your car takes off like a speeding bullet, and as you hit speeds equaling three times the actual speed limit, you then catch right up to the guy that cut you off and then jerk the steering wheel and you start drive onto the wrong side of the road, with oncoming traffic coming your way and all, and then you blast past the Road Rager in your car that has now turned into a deadly rocket of rage, and as you pass the Road Rager, which you are now also, you then extend your arm out of the window and you throw your glass bottle right at the bastard.

You hear a smash, and you are immediately satisfied knowing that you hit their car and the bottle has broken! Revenge is yours! But now, considering you are still driving on the wrong side of the road, you have to swerve back into the right lane and you avoid nearly causing an accident as you almost just went head on into and oncoming car.

As you get back into the right lane, you then look in the rearview mirror and see the Road Rager right on your tail (back bumper) egging you on to pull over and now they are threatening you with hand signal that he wants to fight. Yes, he is showing you his fist and he is waving it around in the air. Hey, you are all green and pumped up, and mad as hell. Why not get out and fight? I have.

Now you and this other manic both pull over, and then you both jump out of your cars and run up to one another and then get in each other's faces.

Next, a few vulgar words are enchained and you both put your fists up and act, that's right, ACT, like you are going to fight. You circle each other bopping back and forth looking like two roosters in a cockfight in some Mexican's backyard and are doing nothing but verbally assaulting one another.

Next thing you know, as you two morons continue your dancing routine right there on the side of the road in broad daylight and put on your free show for the public to see and laugh at, a cop then pulls up and he gets out of his car in a fit of fury and seems more pissed off then the both of you.

The cop walks up to you, and not the guy who started the whole ordeal, and you know what the cop says to you, he says, "You nearly ran me off the road back there, you F****** A** H***, now license and registration!"

When you passed the Road Rager on the wrong side of the road to retaliate and hit him with the bottle, and you almost crashed into the other car head on into that car, it was an unmarked cop car! Nice job, buddy. The Road Rager is just going to get a ticket for disorderly persons, but you are Reckless driving ticket and a disorderly persons! The cop did not see the other guy do anything, therefore he can't write him a moving violation ticket, even though you just told him, "HE STARTED IT!" Cops don't care about that shit; it ain't high school anymore, buddy. Cops want evidence, and they can only charge people for what they see.

You should have never retaliated! When you do you only put yourself on the level of the Road Rager, if not worse, just like in the example story. If you had just controlled your temper, Hulk, and you were able to let it go it would have just been a simple wash of the car. Now you have to go and wash your car, and go to court.

I understand that it is humiliating if someone does something like that to you and no one should be treated that way, but sometimes you have to let it go or things will only get worse for you.

Be Polite No Matter What
There is a method/tactic that I have come up with that will help you to be able to decipher which kind of Road Rager you could be dealing with in your current Road Rage situation. You may be dealing with a

regular Road Rager, or a Road Lunatic. Once you figure this out you will know how much danger you could possibly be in, and you will know what you will have to do to get out of the situation.

If you are dealing with a regular Road Rager, a regular person who is just having a bad day, you will be able to just drive away after a few harsh words and a hand gestures or two. If you are dealing with a Road Lunatic, a person who Road Rages for a living, they might possibly try to follow you home and attack you physically on your front lawn so you want to know this so you can get help or try to get out of this situation before it gets to that point.

The method/tactic that I have come up with to decipher what kind of Road Rager you are dealing with is call the "Be Polite No Matter What" method. Yes, your mother had the right idea. Being polite is better than being mean, and you do get more out of it.

Example Story: You are driving kind of fast down a two-lane road coming home from the supermarket one day and as you are speeding down the road you see a cop up head on the other side of the road. As soon as you see the cop you panic and jam on the breaks and slow down way to fast nearly causing an accident and having the person driving behind you nearly crash right into the back of your car.

You continue to drive pretending you did not do anything wrong and pass the cop doing 20 miles per hour in a 35-mile-per-hour because you are a little chicken and you are afraid of cops. Luckily the cop did not see you jam on your breaks like that.

After passing the cop the car, the car who almost rear ended you now pulls up next to you while you are driving down the road to give you are piece of their mind. They feel like telling you how much of an idiot you are.

The person pulls up next to you and yells, "Hey, J*** O**, where did you learn how to drive!?" "You almost caused a major accident!" "Learn how to F***** drive!"

You feel like lashing back and saying some mean words in return but you decided not to and to be polite no matter what instead, even though they are yelling profanity at you. You yell back, "Oh, I am sorry! I know I am a terrible driver! THANK YOU!" and then kind of laugh.

The driver of the other car gives you a funny look, and says, "Yeah, that's right," and then drives off.

You see, you were polite no matter what, even though they were yelling profanity and trying to make you look stupid and feel bad. Instead you made them feel that way. The person did not know what to say in return because you were polite instead of mean, and you made them feel awkward and made them realize that they were acting foolish and that is not right to begin with.

What you were dealing with there is a Regular Road Rager, not a Road Lunatic. Regular Road Ragers will leave you alone when you are polite to them, they are not crazy and stupid. And when you are polite like that you have a better chance of the Road Rage altercation ending faster and significantly safer.

Now, let's try this story with another person.

Example Story: You are driving kind of fast down a two-lane road coming home from the supermarket one day and as you are speeding down the road you see a cop up head on the other side of the road. As soon as you see the cop you panic and jam on the breaks and slow down way to fast nearly causing an accident and having the person driving behind you nearly crash right into the back of your car.

You continue to drive pretending you did not do anything wrong and pass the cop doing 20 miles per hour in a 35-mile-per-hour because you are a little chicken and you are afraid of cops. Luckily the cop did not see you jam on your breaks like that.

After passing the cop the car, the car who almost rear ended you now pulls up next to you while you are driving down the road to give you are piece of their mind. They feel like telling you how much of an idiot you are.

The person pulls up next to you and yells, "Hey, J*** O**, where did you learn how to drive!?" "You almost caused a major accident!" "Learn how to F****** drive!"

You feel like lashing back and saying some mean words in return but you decided not to and to be polite no matter what instead, even though they are yelling profanity at you. You yell back, "Oh, I am sorry! I know I am a terrible driver! THANK YOU," and then kind of laugh.

The person yells back, "Hey, what are you laughing at, what are you being a F****** wise guy with me!" then the person throws something at your car, and they try to run you off the road. You swerve as to not get hit them and then they continue to chase you and cures at you and this Road Rage will continue to escalate unless you either lose the person or you get help.

You see, you are dealing with a complete Road Lunatic here. They actually think that because you are being polite that you are messing with their heads. You are not acting mean and vulgar in return so they get even more pissed off. That is what crazy people, like Road Lunatics, do when people don't act the way they want you to, they get even more mad because they think you are messing with their head. Road Lunatics want you to Road Rage in return so they can fight with you.

Being polite no matter what is a good tactic to use though to get out of many Road Rage though because only about one out of every thousand Road Rage altercations that you will get into in your life will be against a Road Lunatic like the guy in the second scenario, so be polite because it works 99% of the time. Any Regular Road Rager will go away when you are polite , and the Road Rage altercation will not escalate, but the Road Lunatic will want to take it further and make it escalate farther, and when that happens, the best thing I could say to you is make a quick U-turn and go back and find the cop at that speed trap and ask him for help because Road Lunatics can be very dangerous, and you don't want to fight with them in any case because it will only end ugly.

Call for Help
You are on the phone half the time when you are driving anyhow, right!? It is like that phone is glued to the side of your head or something.

Isn't it also funny, whenever I am stopped at a traffic light and I look over at the car in the land next to me that is stopped also and I see a person in their car alone and they are talking to themselves. They look like they are as crazy as can be, even if they are in a suit and tie. Anyone that talks to themselves when they are in their car looks crazy to me, but then they turn to the side and you see that stupid Bluetooth thing that is attached to their ear and head. It looks like a robotic tumor on their ear, or like a futuristic hearing aid to me, I just don't get it. And I mean, are you really that important that you always need to be talking when you are in your car and driving, because I know I'm not.

So if you are going to be on that phone for half your life like most people are anyhow, put it to good use. The phone is supposed to be there so we can communicate with one other easier, and help make the world a better place. Not to use it to talk to each other for endless hours a day after day about other people's baby mama drama. That is not what the phone was made for, and everyone who is drama free knows it.

So next time you are driving and notice someone Road Raging on the road, not even if it is at you, do the right thing and call the proper authorities and call it in because it could possibly save someone's life.

If you can, try to get close enough to the Road Ragers car so that you can try to get a license plate number. If you cannot, try to get close enough so you can at least get a good visual description of the car so that when you call the police you can tell them what kind of beat-up car the Road Rager was driving.

Example Story: Picture it, you are a forty-eight-year-old, black female who has just gone through a serious divorce, and today, you are going to take a ride to an old friend's house to vent to her about what has been going on in your personal life.

So as you leave, and you head down the highway to your old friend's house in your 1997 black Mercedes Benz, you look ahead in traffic, and as you do, you notice two cars swerving back and forth a few cars ahead of you.

You become kind of nosy and want to see what is going on so you drive a little faster to get closer to the cars to see what the trouble is. As you get closer you see one of the cars take a swipe (or swerve) at the other one and try to run the other person off the road. You are stunned by what you just saw and think about what you should do!

You think to yourself, "Should I stop this from happening, and try to save the day!" "If I do, I could be a hero!" Absolutely not, you female Action Jackson; keep you're a** out of it, because if you get you get involved and you try to drive between these two cars that are fighting, that car might just try to run you off the road to girl. When a Road Rage altercation is already at this point, which is very heated, anyone else that gets involved will only become another opponent to the Road Rager and they will try to take them out also.

The only thing you can do is try to get close enough without getting involved and try to get a good description of the cars involved in the Road Rage altercation, and or maybe even the license plate.

So you drive up and get close enough, and as you look, what do you see, you notice that it is two Road Punks (Young Punks) driving in a black beat-up 1980s Camaro that has tinted windows, and the two punks are messing around with an older man on the road who is driving in an older brown Chevy Caprice.

Guess what, that is good enough and just that is about all the info you will need to be able to describe the cars when you call the police.

And also, try to remember the time you saw the incident, and what highway you were traveling on and by what mile marker you were near. This way when you tell the cops what time, and where you were on the highway when the incident happened, they will be able to estimate by time and speed how far down the highway the Road Ragers in the black Camaro have gotten since the incident has taken place and they can catch them down the road. So call for help rather than call for pizza like you usually do. We all know Gino's Pizza is number one on you speed dial rather than 911....

It is a very common now to call in and report aggressive driving (Road Rage) on the road when it is seen. There are signs all over the interstates in New Jersey and New York telling you to report it when you see it, and the sign has a specific number for you to call rather than just 911. Like they say, until Big Brother has eyes (cameras) everywhere to watch over us and keep us safe, we ourselves have to partake in being those eyes (witness) to what goes on and report it to Big Brother so that we can help keep our community, streets, and ourselves safer.

Drive to a Public Place

This is a good tactic if you want to try to get a Road Rager away from you if they are already in the process of following you. The best thing you can do if you have a Road Rager flowing you is to get to a public place as soon as possible! Getting to a public place during a Road Rage altercation is good for a few reasons.

Number one, get somewhere public and populated fast, and this is so you can get into view of a camera and try to get the Road Rager who is following you on it. If you drive through a busy parking lot, like a Walmart, a bank, a gas station, center of town, 99 percent of the time they will have a camera recording what goes in the vicinity of their property.

If you drive through the parking lot and you catch the Road Rager on camera, following you and being disorderly (throwing things at you, yelling), then you will have hard evidence of them doing and that is very important.

From a camera, you can get the description of the car, maybe a license plate, and the actual offence that they caused to you caught on tape, and that is the most important evidence in court of law besides a confession. Once you have them on camera, you got them "BY THE B***S," basically.

Number two, the public place will be filled with people that can be accountable witnesses to this Road Rager altercation that is taking place in front of them. You know how people are, once they hear some beeping and yelling, everyone starts rubber necking (being nosy), so they can all look to see what is going on). And if they see you being attacked, chased, or yelled at, and it is not caught on a camera, at least you have others witnesses, and they are just as good in court of law, if not better than and actual video.

Number three, if you go somewhere public and highly populated, there might be a security guard or police officer on duty! In some strip malls they sometimes have rent-a-cops (security guards) driving around in a little white truck with a flashing yellow light on top. If you have someone bothering all you have to do is pull up to them and ask for help. Not only is it their job to help you, but they will have a CB/walkie-talkie that they can used to get in contact with the real police immediately.

Another good place you will want to pull up to if a Road Rager is giving you a hard time and following you is a police station! Use your

GPS and find the nearest one and drive right to it. Once you pull up to that police station I promise you that Road Rager will take off like a bat out of hell (really fast). Now you will be able to report the incident and the Road Rager will not be far from the police station and the cops might be able to catch them quicker. If you are lucky, when you pull into the police station there will be a cop outside and you can tell the cop and they will get into their car right away and try to catch the Road Rager. I don't know about you, but every time I drive past my town's police station there is always a cop standing outside looking like he could use something to do!

So if you ever get into a Road Rage altercation and someone is bothering you and you want to get out of it safely, get to a public place quickly. If the Road Rager is not completely crazy, and he has any common sense to him/her, as soon as they see you pull into somewhere public, they will just leave!

Chapter 6

What Is Road Rage Psychology?

This is it! The class that everyone who has ever driven a car should attend, Road Rage Psychology 101 for you kids and adolescent adults who have Road Rage. Right here is real underling main cheese (main reasons) behind why most people Road Rage. Behind every Road Rager there is quite possibly a mental disorder or chemical imbalance that is probably causing them to Road Rage and flip out on the road, and the funny thing is, they don't even know it.

Learning and knowing about the Psychology behind Road Rage will help answer questions and gives reason as to why some of people Road Rage in life, and why some never will. Why a person like me used to Road Rage, and why I don't anymore. Why some people will only Road Rage once in their life, and never again. Why some people need to Road Rage every day. And the one main question, "Why do I Road Rage, I am a mean person on the road, yet in no other aspects in my life am I a mean person?!" That last one is always a big one and nobody really has a good explanation for that question.

While most people think that Road Rage is only caused by anger, if you have anger issues and you go to a psychologist, they will always ask you this question, "Well, what is causing you to be angry?! Is it really just because the guy in front of you cut you off that you are mad and Road Raging at them, or is it really because you had no mother as a child and your father used to abuse you verbally, or is it because you really have a chemical imbalance and a psychological problem and you forgot to take your medication for it today, you know, for your schizophrenia?!" There is almost always more to the situation when someone is angry than just being angry and everyone knows it, including yourself.

So I have put together a list of possible disorders that could be the underlining cause and effect of your Road Rage problem. Hopefully by reading about Road Rage Psychology maybe you can find a reason as to why you are such a bastard to others on the road, yet are a saint to others when you are not in your car and you are walking the streets.

No, you were not born a bad person or born to be angry and mad at everyone. Something happened to you that made you that way. What is it? Hopefully reading into some of this chapter can help you realize what is going on with you and it can maybe steer you in the right direction, instead of you steering your car into oncoming traffic on purpose when people piss you off, and just maybe steering you to an answer instead. An answer that can help you change your ways, and or at least help you realize whether or not you need professional help.

If you do realize that you have a serious Road rage problem that is being caused by and underline mental issues, and you do decide seek out the proper help for it, there is more than a good chance that you can get to the bottom of it and cure it, whatever the case may be. That is if you are willing to! If you want to stay angry and not talk to a psychologist because you don't think that it will do you any good talking to one, then it never will. You have to be willing to change, and most importantly, have to want to change and be willing to do some work to do it!

Intermittent Explosive Disorder

Intermittent Explosive Disorder (I.E.D.) is a behavioral disorder characterized by very an extreme form of anger and rage that takes place in

sudden outbursts! These outbursts of anger and rage are always disproportionate to the size of the situation at hand. Like your friends say,
you always over exaggerate.

It is currently categorized in the Diagnostic and Statistical Manual of
Mental Health Disorders as an impulse control disorder. In other words,
you cannot control your feelings and emotions and you act on impulse,
and it says so in the crazy book. It is also along in the crazy book next to
pyromania, kleptomania, and pathological gambling. Nice to know.

Impulse aggression that is caused by the disorder is mainly un-
premeditated and is defined by a disproportionate reaction to any
provocation, real or perceived. Sometimes people will feel tension, frustration, and mood changes right before an outburst can take place.

To explain this disorder in simpler terms, it is a step under psychotic. You overreact with outbursts of anger and rage all of a sudden
out of nowhere and to any situation, whether it is real or not real!? You
are like a time bomb waiting to go off, but no one knows the time? You
can explode whether you are eating breakfast, doing your job at work,
driving in your car, or just plain out sitting at home doing nothing.

Example Story: You are 24-year-old white female and you are driving along one morning to the supermarket minding your own business
and enjoying the ride. It is a nice day and you have the windows down.
As you are driving along down this two-lane road you have to stop for
a red light.

As you are stopped at the light waiting for it to change a random
person pulls up in the right lane next to you and stops dead even with
you so that you and this person are dead neck (side by side evenly) looking the same way. Yeah, I hate when people do that to me to. What
pulls up next to you is some weird looking nerdy dude with some Coke
bottle (really thick lens) glasses on and a terrible haircut in some beat-
up old car.

As you are looking straight you notice this person out of the corner of your eye kind of looking at you. Actually, after just two seconds you can feel the stare of this person burning the hair off of the side of your head. You get a little curious as to what the person is looking at so you turn your head slightly, not fully, to kind of look at them out of the corner of your eye. As you do they snap their head forward to look straight and avoid eye contact.

You look straight yourself again and kind of get a little uneasy about the situation and start thinking all kind of bad thoughts to yourself. You say to yourself in your head, what the F*** is this guy looking at, is he a pervert or something, what do I got something on my face, and then you start to look in the mirror. Tension builds in your mind, your start to feel anxious about the light changing and getting out of the situation, your leg starts to shake, and then you start to get feelings of anger.

You look to your left to try to focus on something else but it does not work. In your mind you think that he is still staring at you and you are mad about this. You start to think to yourself, "What the F*** is this guy staring at?" "This pervert is going to get it," "That is it!" and then, boom, you explode and go into a fit of violent rage and anger.

Your turn to the side and start yelling like a wild madman out of your passenger car window from your driver's seat at this poor nerdy-looking fella next to you. You say to the nerd, "What the F*** do you keep on looking at, pervert?" "You look over at me one more time, I am going to rip off my steering wheel, get out of my car, and then come over there and ram it down your throat, you four-eyed J***."

All the nerd does is jump back in shock, gasp for air, and pull around the car in front of him and take off running the red light because you frightened him so much with your overly exaggerated outburst of anger and rage that came out of nowhere. That is what we call a case of the Intermittent Explosive Disorder.

You exploded on the poor Nerdy Four-Eyes for no reason. Well, the reason was because you thought, let me say it again, you thought he was staring at you in a perverse manner and you felt threatened and you built that up in your head. All Four Eyes were doing was admiring your nice car. You like to drive in a nice new Ford Mustang to get attention, but yet, when people look at it, you are all like, what the hell are you looking at! Idiots and psychotic people do stuff like that. You have to be a little easier going.

And come on, let's be honest. How many times have you stared a fight in a sports bar because you thought, let me say it again, you thought that somebody was looking at you in a wrong way? You felt threatened, started a huge fight, over exaggerated about the whole thing, like threatened to kill the guy for looking at you wrong and then found out later that the guy was not looking at you at all. He was looking at the baseball game on the TV on the wall behind you.

If you think that you may have this condition, like I used to, this may be a real reason why you Road Rage a lot! This could also be a reason why you explode on everyone from time to time for no reason. Like your friends, your husband, you coworkers, and people who look at you the wrong way in bars.

Intermitted Explosive Disorder is a disorder that does require treatment depending in the severity of the disease. It could require some simple treatment only lasting just a couple of months and maybe just some visits with a psychologist, or if the condition is severe it could require years of treatment from visits with psychologists, psychiatrists, and possible treatment with medication. If your condition is bad and left untreated, you may end up in a straitjacket because of it one day, if you have already not before.

OCD (Obsessive Compulsive Disorder)

The weirdest metal disorder that can possibly be making you Road Rage is if you have any form of OCD, Obsessive Compulsive Disorder. I have mild to moderate OCD myself and know many people that do. This disease can be a real pain in the A** to deal with personally and it can make it very tough on people to manage even very simple tasks in their lives at times. If you don't' believe me, just ask Howey Mandel.

OCD is a mental disorder known as Obsessive Compulsive Disorder. It is an anxiety disorder that is characterized by a series of intrusive thoughts that can lead to, and/or produce certain feelings and emotions like fear, anxiety, nervousness, and worry that are brought on by repetitive behaviors aimed at reducing the associated anxiety, or by a combination of such obsessions and compulsions. Some repetitive symptoms of this disorder can include extreme hording (holding onto a ton of junk), repeated checking (always looking at your watch), excessive cleaning (like those people that wash their hands every five minutes), avoiding certain numbers (look out, 666 is evil), and repetitive violent and/or religious thought patterns (Jesus freaks and dangerous people have the same thought patterns?). This is usually, but not always, accompanied by a series of nervous rituals such as, the constant opening and closing of doors a certain amount of times, having to step on certain things when walking (such as lines or cracks), have to eat your food in certain ways, and even having to drive in certain ways.

I know it sounds crazy, but my OCD would kick in a lot when I was driving. My OCD would kick in and I used to get nervous and then start acting weird when certain cars on the road where not driving the way I wanted them to. I would get very annoyed and then almost frantic when cars would drive in certain spots or certain ways and I would have to check my rearview a thousand times.

When I was driving, if there was even a thought that I had a car driving next to me in my blind spot (driving on the lower left, or right side, side of my car out of view), then I would have to check my side view or look over my shoulder a hundred times until I was absolutely positive that there was not one there. If there was I had to either speed up, or slow down to get them out of my blind spot immediately or I would continue to look to my side. If I could not get them out of my blind spot quick enough I would instantly begin to think that they were doing it on purpose to upset me, and then I would go into panic mode. Once that happened, then I would do whatever it took to remove them from driving near me. Either I would pull over completely and let them pass, or I would wobble my car and move from side to side and pretend that I was drunk so that they would have to back up and stay away from me. I could never, and still cannot, drive with someone in my blind spot for more than two second without it getting me agitated and bugging me out (flipping out) and having to repeat my nervous disorder of looking at the rearview or over my shoulder until I am out of the situation.

A couple of other OCD problems I had that were car related was definitely and obsessive cleaning problem. My car always had to be clean. I never had any junk in my car or truck, even if they were old beat up looking crappy cars. They used to look like crap from the outside, but they were nice and clean on the inside. If I dropped a friend off and they left an empty Snapple bottle in my back seat or something, they would get a phone call as soon as I seen the bottle and they would get reprimanded for leaving junk in my car. I hated that. I don't know how people can drive around with junk flopping around in their car and making noises like that and not even notice it. That is one compulsion problem, I cannot drive with junk rolling around in my back seat. If I am driving and I hear junk bouncing around in my car, I will pull over immediately and throw it out.

The other obsessive cleaning problem was that I could never drive with dirt on my windshield. If I was driving and I got hit with a bomb of bird crap I would continually look at it and let it bother me until it was clean, so I would have to pull over immediately and clean it up if I had some Wendy's or McDonald's napkins on me.

A friend of mine also had an OCD problem that was driving related and it is pretty funny. Whenever he uses to drive over manhole covers, if the cover did not go under the center of the car when he was driving and went under for say, the right side, then he would then have to make sure that next time he drove over a manhole cover that it would have to go under the left side of the car! He told me that it felt more even in his brain that way. No joke.

As if you did not know, like most problems in life, you don't realize that you have problem or developed one until someone else tells you of course. A coworker had to say to me one day, "Bro, maybe you got some OCD or something because you are way to clean and organized to be a dude!" At the time I really did not even know what OCD really was, but of course being curious and half a hypochondriac also, I had to look it up right away on the internet away. After reading up about it online I took a long hard look at myself, guess what I saw.

I have to wake up at a certain time or I feel as if my whole day will be thrown off. I have to have everything in order in my room ALL the time. All my music is in alphabetical order, close folded, and paperwork on my desk always has to be straight. I eat and take my vitamins in a certain order. If I do not take them in a certain order I don't tend to feel the results from them as good I think, and that the vitamins won't work right. I sleep a certain way, only in two different spots. I poop at a certain time. I only eat certain foods, and in certain ways and order. My clothes have to fit a certain way. If they don't I will throw them out.

I like my sex a certain way. And guess what, I drive in a certain way! "Wow," I said to myself, "I guess I really do have a case of OCD!"

I never did seek professional help for my disorder because I guess as if I never really felt like it was a major issue, so I guess I am kind of like they say, self-diagnosed and still active with the disease. I am kind of okay living with my OCD for what it is worth and I think it is what makes me such a clean and organized person.

If you feel like you could possibly have OCD, though, and it does interfere with your life, whether at work, at home, or especially on the road! Then I would seek some help.

The help for OCD can vary also by the severity of the disease. You can get help for the condition just by seeking professional counseling, and they will help you to deal with it yourself without medication. Or, if your condition is severe enough, you would have to seek out a good psychiatrist who can put you on medication that will help you with symptoms of the disease.

That is, unless you kind of like OCD like I do and you feel like you can use it to your advantage so it to can make you a better person like me, then go for it. Live in the active disease as they say and make it work for you.

So look out, Leonardo DiCaprio, the man who has to step on every piece of gum that is on the floor when he walks down the street! I got you beat, bro. I have an OCD compulsion about running over and aiming for every paper cup or plastic bottle I see roaming the streets when I am driving down the road. Leonardo can just say excuse me with his OCD disorder and step on his gum. Me, I almost nearly cause a major accident every time I see a paper cup because I want to run it over!

Type-A Personality

Originally published in the early 1950s, the Type-A personality and

Type-B personality theory (also known as the Jacob Goldsmith theory) is a theory that was created so that it could describe two main contrasting personality traits that human people may have.

First we have the **Type-A personality**. People who have a Type-A personality are described as the more ambitious, aggressive, businesslike, impatient, preoccupied, time conscious, and tightly wound humans. You know, the businessman who is always in a rush.

Then we have the **Type-B personality**. People with the Type-B personality are basically described as the exact opposite of the Type-A. The Type-B personality people are more, relaxed, levelheaded, patient, calm, cool, and as they say easygoing kind of human. You know, I am going to the beach and carrying a surfboard.

So who are you, or should I say, what personality are you? Are you a businessman that lives his life in the fast lane? Do you run out the door at 7:00 A.M. not even eating breakfast and chugging a gallon of espresso instead? Do you hop into your Chevrolet Corvette and race for the office at 125 miles per hour looking at your watch a thousand times to make sure you will get there at exactly 7:25 A.M. like you do every morning? And if things do not go according to plan, like you get stuck in traffic and run late, are you the first one to beep the horn out of the other one hundred fifty cars sitting next to you in traffic? Is that you?

Or are you the guy the takes his time in the morning and actually eats breakfast like a normal human being? Are you the kind of person who hops into his 1965 Convertible Mustang and puts the top down before you head to work at your little diner that you own near the beach? Do you not even look at your watch when you head to work, rather than look at the sunrise? And when you get stuck in traffic on the way to work, do you just laugh about it because you know all the back roads to work? Is that you?

So let me ask you again, which personality do you think you are? Now, after you have decided which personality type you are, let me ask you, how often do you Road Rage!?

I will bet you the pink slip(title) to my car that if you have said to yourself that you are a Type-A personality that your Road Rage is a hundred times worse than a Type-B personality.

Yeah, I know, it sucks, but that is just the way it is and that is just the way it is going to be unfortunately because that is how you are programed. The personality says so.

I will definitely go out on limb here and tell you that I was born a Type-A personality. I was always, very aggressive, very impatient, and very tightly wound as they say. Even though I was never really businesslike or preoccupied. It was more like I was a Type-A-B personality. It was like I was always in a rush, but had to nowhere to go. I would Road Rage at people and scream at them to get out of my way like I had somewhere important to go, but I was not really doing anything besides going to the mall to get some food!

Now, I would tell you to go and get help for your Type-A personality problem, but unfortunately, there is no real help that you can seek for this personality and this is why. This is not a disorder. This is who you are, your actual personality.

You would have to change the way you think, the way you act, and basically, who you are. You would have to go from a Type-A to Type-B and I do not even know if that is possible. That is like trying to change a cokehead (cocaine user) to a pothead (marijuana user). I don't even know if it is possible.

But I will tell you this, this theory (the Jacob Goldsmith theory), however simple it is, though, has actually been beat down on by scientists, mathematicians, psychologists, universities and just about everyone else that has a say on the human behavior. No one likes the Type-A and Type-B personality theory really and it has actually been claimed obsolete in the Health Psychology and in the Medical Psychology field so all in all I guess you really don't have to worry about this at all.

The reason why no one likes this theory is because there are so much more to human personalities then to just fit them into two simple categories. The human personality is far more complex than that. The reason why I still mentioned it, is because I know for a fact that if they still used this method to determine someone's personality traits, and they were classified as a Type-A-personality, and they asked them how often they Road Raged and asked someone who is a Type-B, the results would be 250 percent higher. Type-A-personalities would Road Rage at a much higher percentage than a person who is a Type-B-Personality.

Multiple Personality Disorder

This one is for all you Road-Raging superheroes out there. Multiple Personality Disorder is a dissociative disorder which is characterized by a separation from one's self and their consciousness from time to time. Usually, there are just two personalities within the person that have this disorder, the guy we all know to be normal at work (Dr. Jekyll), and then the one who pops out at all the holiday parties (Mr. Hyde), but there can be more than two personalities in some rare and extreme cases.

When it comes to Multiple Personality Disorder there is the usually the first personality. The main one, the one we all know that is the more conservative, quiet, normal, and kind of dull personality.

Then there is the second personality. The one that is made up for the multiple. The one we have never seen before. It is the more impulsive, bare, outrageous, and uninhibited personality!

Multiple Personality Disorder is almost always a response to a case of extreme stress in one's life. It is a very rare disorder and is very hard to diagnose and treat and most psychologists have not even been able to treat the disorder with a high success rate yet.

Your normal self (the guy we all know) might not be able to understand this disorder, but I am sure if I got to talk your other personality (the guy we never seen before), Captain Road Rage, I am 100-percent sure he would understand it.

You see, most of us are born with somewhat normal lives, and try as best as we can to lead out normal lives for as long as we can if possible. We all want to go to grow up with loving parents and have a good home life, go to a nice school, grow up and get a good job, have a loving wife or husband, have some beautiful kids with positive attitudes (good luck with the positive attitude part), and then retire to a condominium in Florida with a good pension and Social Security check and live out the rest of lives soaking up the sun. Amen to the American Dream.

Almost all of us are programed to believe this and want this for ourselves in life. It is almost everyone's dream to live a happy and normal life and to go through the process without a problem. There is no reason why every single one of us cannot have this, until that reason shows up.

When we are going through this process and a traveling down the easy road of life and a reason/situation comes along that tries to, or does, messes it up, whether the situation is big or small, it can act as a roadblock that will either cause us to stop or throw us of track. Some of us, once faced with this dilemma of a roadblock going down what was a pretty easy road of life caused by this situation/reason, if we do not know what to do it can cause major stress. To deal with the stress and to get passed this roadblock and to get back on course, we may need certain emotions to get passed it, certain feelings that we (the guy we all know) may have never even used, felt, or tapped into before because he always had an easy life, such as confidence, strength, rage and anger. And since most of us don't know how to feel those feelings because we never did before, we are scared to use them. You have been a certain way (calm, dull) your whole life and you are afraid to change and feel those feelings (courage, rage) so in response, your brain makes up a buddy/friend/another person completely inside the same body who will help you feel those feelings for you so that you can get passed the roadblock and get yourself farther down the road of life to where we need to be, amen. I know, that was a hard one to swallow.

The situation we can be presented with at times can be extreme, just like in the story of Batman. When Bruce Wayne was a child his parents were robbed at gunpoint and killed. You can only imagine the amount of stress put on the boy when he even had to fathom thinking about growing up his whole life without his parents and what could have happened to him without them. His process of an normal life was shattered, or was it. The normal, quiet, kind of dull boy known as Bruce Wayne developed a Multiple Personality Disorder over time to deal with the stress of not having parents. He, or his brain or subconscious mind, made a whole other personality, one that is impulsive, brave, and kind of uninhibited, called Batman!

This situation that presented Bruce Wayne as a child with stress is very severe, but yet, his Multiple Personality known as Batman is however positive, thank God.

Your situation though is not at severe but it still is pretty bad and the Multiple Personality Disorder that you have created to deal with the stress in your life is a little more negative.

Example Story: You are a 40-year-old white man, and you whole life you have been a quiet, dull, boring, pushover who never bothers anyone, you know, kind of like the mild-mannered Bruce Banner.

Growing up, you had great plans for your life, such as being happily married until you die, your kids were supposing follow in your foot steps and take over the family store, and you were supposed to retire to

Florida. Unfortunately, things have not bene going the way you have planned and everything you hoped for when you were younger has pretty much gotten tossed out the window as your daughter is pregnant at the age of seventeen, your son was just kicked out of high school for using drugs and alcohol at the age of sixteen, you and your wife are getting a divorce and she is taking the two kids that let you down with her, and the condo that you invested money into in Florida is a flop and you can't even sell it now and you lost you whole investment which was over 200,000$.

Now, because you are going through all these situations at once, you have now been confronted with a ton of roadblocks on what was supposed to be and easy road of life, so you have been going through a ton of stress lately because of it and you do not know how to deal with. Hey, no one knows teaches you how to deal or be prepared for a divorce, some trouble making kids, and bankruptcy. These are all part of the school of life my friend.

So because you have been under so much pressure and stress lately, and not knowing how to deal with it, your subconscious mind eventually did something, it made or developed a Multiple Personality Disorder to deal with all the stress. You mind made a personality that is a little more aggressive, bare, uninhabited, angry, one that sure as hell isn't no pushover!

You were not aware of this new guy until this new personality showed up in the last two fights that you and your wife had at home recently and in the process of you two arguing she yelled, "I never seen you act like this before, or turn that color before!" You know, a personality called the Incredible Hulk! Unfortunately, this Multiple Personality Disorder is a little more negative that you have created that that of the one Bruce Banner created or came up with. I know, Marvel vs DC.

I would tell you to try to seek out professional help for your Multiple Personality Disorder, but I did write down earlier that it is very hard to diagnose, and almost harder to treat, so I would not suggest going to your psychologist office in your Batman or Superman outfit and say, "Hey Doc, can you help me with my Multiple Personality Disorder!?" They might not only help you with your Multiple Personality Disorder, but they might put you away for a while for being psychotic.

The only thing I can say, though, is this. If your Multiple Personality Disorder is a little more negative and is kind of like the Incredible Hulk, you have to do what he did. You have to learn how to tame, control, that other personality (the Incredible Hulk) like Bruce Banner did. Yes, it took a long time but he did do it and look how he turned out. His Multiple Personality Disorder was crazy and out of control at the beginning, but he turned out to be one of the greatest and strongest superheroes of all time in the end.

Now, "How does Multiple Personality Disorder show up in Road Rage," you ask? Multiple Personality Disorder and Road Rage kind of works like this. This disorder I think answers the question to "Why do some people Road Rage, yet show now other signs of anger or rage anywhere else in their lives?" It is like they are the friendliest people in the world in person, at work, at home, when walking through the store, but yet you bump into them on the road and get into a Road Rage altercation with them and they might get out of their car and pull a tire iron on you, and it won't be to help you change your tire. It will be to bust your windows through and put some dents in the side of your car, and maybe your head if you are lucky enough.

"Why is this," you ask? Some people cannot, let me say it again, cannot handle the stress that they are confronted with on the road for some reason?! Road Rage altercations (people beeping, yelling, screaming at them) is a situation that presents more stress for them than any other situation for some reason!? And when they are confronted with this situation and feel that stress, that it when you see them turn to their Multiple Personality Disorder (Captain Road Rage) to deal with it. It is the only logical explanation for why some people Road Rage, yet show no other forms or rage at all anywhere else in their lives.

Yes, your Multiple Personality Disorder created a man that I like to refer to as Captain Road Rage. Whenever you are presented with stress on the road it is like you are a completely different person. You slip out of your consciousness and Captain Road Rage takes over! Don't worry and don't feel embarrassed, there are many other people out there in the world who have the same exact Multiple Personality Disorder buddy that just shows up when they are driving.

Claustrophobia
This is an easy one to describe. Claustrophobia is a fear of getting caught in a small or confined space such as a room with no windows, closet, elevator, basement, plain, train, and yes, even a car! It is classified as an anxiety disorder and usually results in hyperventilating and major panic attacks.

It is not necessarily so that the person who has claustrophobia is afraid of the room, closets, elevators, cars, plains, but rather they are afraid if they could get confined to the area and caught in a situation where they could lose the oxygen in that particular place and they would suffocate.

For say, if they get caught in room with no windows and someone shuts and locks the door on them. A person with claustrophobia would instantly bug out (have a panic attack) and try to rip the door off the hinges so they could get out of the room. If they cannot get the door open, within seconds they would believe that they are losing air and suffocating, even if they are not, and would then start to rip clothes off of themselves because they feel as if they get air when they do that and it relieves tension. Then they would start to hyperventilate, and probably pass out unless you opened up the door! Yeah, real funny joke, jerk. You know your buddy is going to kick your ass for that.

It is said that anywhere from 4 percent to 6 percent of the whole world could have claustrophobia, but not even half of that seeks or gets help for it, they just live with it. In severe cases of claustrophobia some people cannot even get MRIs done or be in large crowds, even if they are outside at a concert.

But I think you know what I am going to get at. Let's talk about the not so severe cases of claustrophobia and the ones who have panic attacks in cars!

Example Story: You are an 18-year old girl, is a Friday afternoon, it is summertime, you just got out of work, and you just got paid. You know what the means don't you, time to head to the beach! You cash your check, head home to grab a bathing suit and get out of your work clothes, then you stop at the gas station to get gas and some snacks for the tip ahead, and then get on the highway to head down the shore.

You take off onto the highway like a bat out of hell, and then you turn on the radio to set the mood as it is about a two-hour ride down the beach. You enjoy the day and your ride as it is beautiful outside, and you make good timing as traffic and the road have been very good to you for the most part, but then about an hour into the ride you get gasp as you see traffic up ahead. You approach the traffic by hitting your breaks and then slowing down, and then you get stuck in dead-stop traffic, and I mean, it aren't going nowhere. Your car is parked! There is a major accident up ahead but you don't know that and you are nowhere even near it. You have two miles of traffic in front of you.

Now, as you pull up into traffic and come to a dead stop you sit there for only about thirty seconds and you start to feel irritated and start to panic a little bit about the thought of being stuck there for too long and not being able to get out.

Right away you look around for a way out, but there is no way out. You got stuck right in the middle lane of the three lane highway in between two 18-wheelers. One to the left of you and one to the right of you. Beautiful, I know. As soon as you become aware of how stuck you really are, you feel the pressure start to build in your car and then in your head as you start to panic. At only one minute you start to roll all the windows down and you start to huff and puff. Next, you start to take some clothes so you can cool down, and then you turn the radio off completely because it is agitating you and you want to think of a way out! You look around for a way out and you start to breathe heavily and get dizzy a little bit. At only two minutes into this whole ordeal, you get out of your car, something you are not supposed to do mind you, so you can look ahead to see what is the hold up. As soon as you get out of the car you feel relieved! You stand outside looking like a weirdo because you are the only one out of your car, so people give you funny looks. You know people are looking at you and you don't care You stand out of your car for about a minute, and try to stay there for as long as possible because you know that as soon as you sit back in your car you will start to panic.

As you stand there in the middle of the road standing by your car in the middle of dead stop traffic, you suddenly hear cop sirens and then you look behind you to see that it is cop car coming up the emergency lane heading toward the accident ahead of you. Wisely, you get back into your car because you don't want the cop to see you standing in the middle of the road because you will get into trouble, so you jump back in, and wait for him to pass by. As he does, you stay in your car hoping that he will get to the accident quickly so that the traffic will move.

As you get back into your car, your nervousness comes right back within one minute. You start to huff and puff again, and then you really panic and as you quickly realize now that traffic really isn't going anywhere, because as you look at the highway exit a mile ahead of you, you now see a fire truck getting onto the highway. You got about another hour before anyone can go anywhere, but that isn't your problem because after one more minute you go into full on panic mode and then you jump back out of your car because you can't breathe. You have made a decision that you have to get out of being in-between these two tractor trailer because you feel like you are going to be crushed, and you need to get your car out of that traffic and you need to get off of the highway because you can't think. You are feeling faint, and in a state of mental anguish and panic, you make a desperate attempt to get out of your situation so you resort to drastic measures. Now everyone looks over at you as you actually leave your car and then walk over and knock on the side of the18-wheelers' doors that is to the right of you.

The truck driver sitting in his truck is dumbfounded that he hears a knock on the side of his truck, and when the driver looks, he sees a young girl that is half naked and sweaty that has panic in her eyes, and before he can even say anything, you ask the driver of the 18-wheeler if he can move his truck out of the way so you can move your car and get out. The truck driver replies with "Well, I can't really do that, honey," and as soon as he is done talking, that response makes you flip out. Now you grab the bar, climb up onto the side of the 18 wheeler and you point your finger in the trucks drivers face and you yell at him and say, "If you don't move your truck, Bob Segar, I will rip you out of your seat and do it myself!" Bob Segar jumps back and gasps, and he sees how nervous and angry you really are and fears that you will live up to your word, or worse, might possibly bite off his leg, if he does not do what you ask. Bob Segar does not say another words and then he puts his truck in gear and then starts to moves his truck over into the emergency lane so you can get your car out.

You jump off of the side of his truck and then you hop back into your car and take off like a madman doing 85 miles per hour speeding down the emergency lane and getting off at the next exit even though you don't know where it takes you, just as long as there is no traffic and you are free to move!

Now that is what I would definitely call case of the car anxiety because of claustrophobia. If this has ever happened to you, you definitely need to go talk to a doctor about your claustrophobia. It would seem as if a lot of people in life could be car claustrophobic at times, but it takes more so take a longer period of time for most people to go into a panic attack mode of that severity. I would say that even a person with a short fuse and has a bad temper that seems to Road Rage quite often, like me and you, can last at five to ten minutes in traffic before getting out of our car and asking people to move. Normal people who don't Road Rage often, I would say can last even up to fifteen to thirty minutes before they start flipping out and beeping and yelling at other people. But people with claustrophobia can't even last but two minutes in a car without flipping out and Road Raging at people, as you can see in the story.

Car claustrophobes can only drive in free-flowing traffic they say, not in traffic that is stuck. As long as their car is moving and it is not stuck somewhere, they will be fine for the most part, but put them in dead-stop traffic and it could end up in a full-on claustrophobia attack with them hyperventilating and maybe even passing out if they don't jump out of the car or get their car out of that traffic jam.

So, if you are a car claustrophobe and you do have to drive, there is only one thing to say to you: "Don't drive anywhere near big cities if you don't want to get stuck in traffic!" Traffic is the norm in big cities, and you and I both know that. If you don't want to get stuck in traffic and you don't want to have another panic attack because you are stuck between two big rigs, then do me a favor and buy a house somewhere in the Midwest where traffic does not even exist and go live out there. The most traffic you will run out there is being stuck behind a farm tractor or cows crossing the road. The only other advice I could give you is if you do have to go to a place where there is a lot of potential traffic that you could get stuck in, either let someone else drive, or take public transportation or walk.

Adrenaline Junkie

This disorder gives answer to the question "Why do people that Road Rage always have to drive over 100 miles per hour every time they get angry?!" The answer, you are addicted to the rush baby, and you don't know how to quit it. You know, kick the habit.

Adrenaline Junkies are people who like to favor (aim for) situations and activities that have more excitement and present more of a rush accompanied with them, rather than less exciting. Hence, they favor the rush, and like a junkie, they need their fix (their source of adrenaline for the day), and they need it now.

Now a lot of people think that to be an adrenaline junkie you have to be some kind of super mountain climber, extreme bungee jumper, crazy skydiver, or a high-risk bank robber to be an adrenaline junkie, and that you have to do these things every day religiously. You know, kind of like that movie *Point Break* with Patrick Swayze and Keanu Reeves. You think that they wake up in the morning, walk into your bathroom, look in the mirror, slap themselves in the face a few times, snort ten lines of cocaine off the vanity, and then go drive to the airport and jump out of an airplane, land on the roof top of a bank, and then rob it all by lunch time. While this may be true for a few, this is definitely not the case for all adrenaline junkies.

There are all types of adrenaline junkies. They can range anywhere from very, very severe as mentioned in the case above to where they have to do crazy things every day like jump off of bridges and wrestle with alligators, to the very moderate cases that are actually hard to pinpoint, where all they do is find situations with drama in them.

A small example of a less severe case of a person being an Adrenaline Junkie would be kind of like your ex-girlfriend and how she uses to sleep with all your buddies behind your back. That was her adrenaline rush. When she was sleeping with them and the thought of her getting caught was a rush. Then every time you would find out that she was sleeping with one of your buddies, you would start a fight with her and then go punch you buddy in the face. She got a kick, high, an adrenaline rush when she was cheating, and then another one when you would fight over her and she loved it. Yes, it sounds crazy, but it is true.

Or what about your poor father? Your mother spent your father's whole retirement on lottery tickets at the corner store! She made the Indian dude at the 7/11 rich and gave all your fathers hard earned money from over thirty years of trying to save what little bit he had right back to the government. Talk about painful one to think about. That crazy bat of a mother of yours got a high, kick, jump, an adrenaline rush every time she scratched out twenty-five Win for Life tickets in a row. And she did that every day for three years. That comes out to 98,815 dollars gone like the wind, and that isn't no drama movie, this is real and I know a person that it happened to.

That is how those adrenaline junkies get their rush, but for you and me, my friend, you can already guess where we get our fix, our high, our rush of adrenaline from that we need every once in a while, to keep us satisfied. That is right, you guessed it, **Road Rage**!

Road Rage has to be one of the most potent forms of releasing adrenaline if you ask me. Road Rage has all the characteristics that you need to make adrenaline jump to an all-time high.

Usually when Road Rage happens, speeding is involved. Most people can get their fix of adrenaline for the day off of that thrill alone, just ask a race car driver. Speeding is exhilarating. Now go and throw in all the other things in there that are involved in Road Rage, such as verbal fighting. That can make a temper jump and adrenaline starts to pump like crazy.

Feeling threatened, or like you are in danger makes your adrenaline pump at full force. For instance, if someone is chasing you in a Road Rage altercation, and you think that maybe the person wants to fight physically, forget about it! Besides jumping out of a plain, I think fighting would be number two on the scale of what releases the most adrenaline. Think about how pumped you used to get when you were a kid and you were ready to go and fight behind the school. You never felt adrenaline like that and felt that alive.

And on that last note, that is what adrenaline does to you. It makes you feel alive for a while. We all find our situations that we are familiar with and get accustomed to that releases this adrenaline, and when we find this, that is where and why we go back to it again and again to get our fix. One person jumps out of plains over and over, another gambles over and over, and another person Road Rages over and over again. We find, choose, and then get accustomed to the situation that best releases our Adrenaline, and then we keep going back to it like a junkie.

But the thing about being an adrenaline junkie is that it is not bad for you, if you know what you are actually doing. For instance, people that jump out of planes most of the time know what they are after and there are many safety measures involved. In fact, many more people die each year in car accidents then skydiving. In fact, the numbers are unreal. Maybe two people die each year skydiving while there are thousands of deaths on the road, and nearly a quarter of a million injuries.

It is crazy. You have more of a chance getting killed in a car accident on the way to work than you do if you jump out of a plain once year, but that is not the point. When people skydive they are doing dangerous things but they are using safety precautions.

When you gamble there are no safety precaution. You have to know your limits. Only the limits you set for yourself. You can bet ten dollars and say that is it, or you can bet the keys to your house and lose it in a flash. It is up to you.

Also, when it comes to Road Rage, there are no safety precautions. Once you start to go over the speed limit and mess around with other people on the road, whether it be yell at them verbally, beep the horn, and take your eyes off the road, you have not only lost all safety by not obeying the rules of the road (the laws), but you put your life, and worse, others' lives in danger by doing so.

Road Rage is definitely one way to get your adrenaline fix, but I would say it is the most dangerous one out of all the ways to try to get it and you should pick a different one. That is if you want to live a long life. Like I said, you got more of a chance at living a longer life if you pick up skydiving as a hobby from what I heard.

Face Value and Restaurant Manners

Now, why most of this chapter is based on some actual clinical psychology that could give you the reason behind why people, or yourself, tends to Road Rage, this next one is actually some street psychology that could help you stop Road Raging in your life. Only thing, though, is that this is not textbook (school) psychology. This is more along the line of street psychology if you will. Something people know that are along the lines of common sense, street smarts, and plain out human manners that pertain to the way we act and why we do what we do rather than it always being a psychological problem or disorder. This is something, we have all done before and we are all susceptible to if we are not careful. Check it out.

The two things I would like to mention partake in Road Rage is something called Face Value and Restaurant Manners. These two go together very well I think (like a match made in heaven). Face value and restaurant manners are two very good reasons why we react like animals in our cars to one another, yet act like very kind and formal human beings to each other when we are not in our cars.

Example Story: You are hungry today and decide to stop at a fast food because you are in a rush, as usual. You live in America and in Northern New Jersey, and that is all people do, rush. You are just going to run into McDonald's and grab a chicken salad and a diet soda because you are on a diet (cough/bulls***). You actually decide to walk into the restaurant today instead of using the drive-thru. That is a healthy change of pace my friend, a diet and walking now. I am proud of you.

But all sarcasm aside, there you are, standing in line minding your own business and waiting like a good person should to order your food like everyone else and looking at the overhead menu when something unusual happens. As you are standing their minding your own business, boom, all of a sudden Big Bertha (a really, really, real big woman) decides to cut in front of you in line and pretend like she doesn't even see you standing there.

You notice what just happened and kind of dwell on the situation for a second and you get a little upset. You were almost going to say something nasty to the rude person who just cut you off for what they did, but you stopped yourself and decide to not to say anything.

But for what reason? Why did not say anything to her?! If you want to know the reason, this is it. You did not say anything to Big Bertha because of something called restaurant manners! You did not say anything to her because you do not want to embarrass that person publicly, or more importantly, yourself. You really don't need to be seen having a verbal argument at McD's with Big Bertha over who is going to get their Big Macs with double cheese, super-sized fries, and diet soda first, do you?

You also did not say anything because you know in your mind that Big Bertha has no face value. She is just a rude person and a lowlife so why even bother, it is just a waist of your time and you know that you are better than that. People that have no face value just means that they have no class, no manners, no worth to them. Their face is worthless in simpler terms.

Also you did not say anything to her because you were afraid that she might eat you instead of her double cheeseburger.

So being this all makes sense today correct, but now we go back to yesterday when you were driving down the road and you got into a Road Rage altercation. What was up with that? Why did that happen? Let's find out.

Example Story: There you are, driving to your parents' house to go help do some housework (chores) like you usually do, because you were brought up the right way unlike most people.

As you are driving along to your parents' house all of a sudden you are cut off by a Speedy Gonzalez as this person comes whipping around the corner running a stop sign and cutting right in front of you in his pimped out little Honda (you know, the ones that sound like lawnmowers).

As soon as you are cut off, you don't even think twice and then you flip out and start yelling and beeping the horn and going crazy at his person that just cut you off. You starting yelling obscene curse words at them and your restaurant manners fly right out your driver-side window along with your middle finger, and maybe your glass bottle of iced tea that is aimed for Speed's Honda. Also, thoughts are going through your mind about you ramming him right off the road with your minivan and catapulting him right over the sidewalk and onto someone's front lawn right where that lawnmower belongs!

What happened? Why are you flipping out on Speedy Gonzalez but not Big Bertha?!

When we are in our cars our manners tend to fade away because we can no longer see a person for face value. We do not get to see the other person's face, so therefore we just see another object in our way of what we are doing and not a person. We actually get angry at the object in our way, not necessarily the person. It is nothing against Speedy himself. You just want to remove his pimped out S*** BOX (ugly car) that just cut you off.

You have to think, had Speed Gonzalez cut you off in line in a person-to-person situation (like at the mall) and you were able to see him face to face, would you flip out on him like that in person? I bet 100 percent not.

You have to remember your restaurant manners when you get into these situations and think to yourself that you are better than that. Yes, I know you are not in a restaurant but you still have to think of the concept the same. You would not want someone you know to see you having it out (fighting) in McD's with Bertha, nor on the side or the road with Speedy Gonzalez going punch for punch in a Road Rage altercation, would you? Both situations are just as bad for your reputation in town, and you know that.

Drive-Walk Associative Syndrome

Now this is a Psychology Theory that I came up with myself. It is not and actual disorder, or condition that even exists, so you cannot go look it up in the crazy book just yet for the definition on it. Well, not at least until they do some research on it and then decide to classify it. Rather this is just a theory that I already gave a name to. It is a theory on a possible syndrome that people have that could also explain why people drive like they do.

A theory is if I had time and money I would put some paperwork together and present it to some first-rate universities to do studies on it. And if they found it interesting enough to actually do studies on and did, I bet you they would find that I am 100-percent right on the money.

It is theory that explains a possible disorder/syndrome in people that makes people drive like they do, and I call it Drive-Walk Associative Syndrome. My best explanation on how to describe this syndrome in very simple terms in this: People drive exactly how they walk. Let me explain now in further detail.

Everything that we do in life is a direct extension of our personalities. The way we dress, the way we eat, the way we talk, the way we act, the way we walk, and also something that many people do not realize, the way we drive. Also, not only the way we do things, but how we do them, why we do them, and the motives for doing them have something to do with our personalities.

You know, fast people eat fast food. Relaxed, laid-back people actually take their time to cook food and chew it when they eat. Adrenaline junkies do cocaine. Hippies smoke week. Flashy women wear skimpy clothes. Conservative women wear a lot of clothes. Drama queens live their life full of emotion. Hermits (people that stay in the house all the time) stay away from situations that are dramatic. Achievers aim for really high goals. Norms (normal people) just settle. Musclemen drive muscle cars. Nice easygoing hippies drive VW Bugs. Big Blue-collar men drive big trucks. Fast paced business men drive fast-paced cars. And so on and so on, you get the point.

But the biggest relation that I have noticed to something that is also is an extension of our personality that is related exactly to how we drive is the way we walk. However, a person walks is exactly how they drive.

I came up with this relation and noticed it years ago. The first person that ever made me notice it was my father. Here is a man that makes almost no mistakes when he walks. He never bumps into things. He never drops things. He is always alert. He does not stumble, even when he is carrying things. He never falls for some odd reason. The man has fallen once since I have been alive and that is almost thirty years. He walks at a normal pace.

Now, if I associate the way this man walks to the way he drives, hence the name Drive-Walk Associative Disorder the similarity is identical.

He drives as professional as can be. He is always alert. He never swerves. He never bumps into anything when he drives such as curbs, other cars, parking humps, poles, shopping carts, or fences. He has maybe been in two accidents in his sixty years of driving and neither of them were his fault, and they only happened because they were completely unavoidable. He does not get into fender benders. He has not gotten a moving violation in over thirty years. He never gets pulled over. If he does it is because he has a light out, not because of the way he is driving. He drives at a normal rate of speed.

Now I will relate this syndrome to an old buddy of mine. This friend of mine was as clumsy as the day is long. He was a big clumsy ox and he could not walk for the life of him. There was not a day that we were not walking through the park and the kid did not trip over something. He could not walk downhills at all. He would have to walk side to side on a slant as to not lose his balance. He always bumped into things. He always stumbled. He always dropped things. He was not even able to run. That was completely out of the question.

If I tell you how he drives, you will not even believe it. He is still one of the only men that I know at thirty years old that does not drive. He has tried to get his license over three times, but unfortunately, every time he hired a driver instructor to help him, he got into an accident.

Now the list can go on and on if you take notice to it in life. If you see an old person walking slowly, they move at 1 mile per hour. If you see how they drive, they go 1 mile per hour. If you see a young person walking through a store that is fast-paced and cutting people off, if you see how they drive, they are will be doing the same exact thing, driving at a fast pace and cutting people off. If you see a really heavyset (nearly obese) person walking and moving at a really slow rate of speed and kind of bumping into people because they are too big and cannot avoid it, the same thing is going on when they drive, I guarantee it, they will drive at a slow rate of speed and bump into things. And the list can go on and on when we take a close look at it.

So this theory I have come up with is no rocket science, but merle something that I think that because I gave a name to, Drive-Walk Associative Disorder, now we can help the people that have it. I consider this as a step toward a cure to bad driving and maybe even Road Rage!

The theory on my cure for people that have this condition is this, if there is a really bad driver and they need help learning how to drive, I say how about we improve how they walk first rather than how they drive!?!? Just maybe if they could walk better, be more coordinated that way, we could help make them a better driver.

Chapter 7

Do You Have Cop Rage?

Well, we all know that, as a result of Road Raging and aggressive driving comes many, many run-ins with police officers! And along with running into these police officers also comes many, many pieces of white or yellow paper, called tickets! And along with many tickets, comes many points on your driver's license (plus surcharges), many tips to the local court house, and sometimes, just sometimes, many a night in a holding cell if you were going fast enough and or pissed the cops off just enough to take you in. This is all a result of Road Rage, and that is a fact.

But what I want to know from you is this. Was it just your Road Raging escapade on the Road that day that got you pulled over and got you those tickets, or is it because you have Cop Rage also!?

Was it just because you were speeding down the road and Road Raging at somebody that got you pulled over and got you five tickets instead of two, got your car impounded, and got you thrown in a holding cell for a night? Or was it because when you were pulled over for that incident and the cop asked you for your license and registration, you responded by yelled in the cop's face and then you told him to, "Go F*** himself!"?

Sure, just about everyone has been speeding in their car on their way home from work and gotten pulled over for it has gotten a ticket or two in their day. Sure, just about everyone has gotten pulled over and given a cop a hard time because they did not feel that they should have been pulled over in the first place. Everyone has a right to stand their ground if they feel they are innocent, but NO, NOT everyone yells in the cop's face, rips up the tickets that they just got handed, and then curses and spits at them!

And that type of behavior, my friend, is what I like to refer to as Cop Rage, sweetheart! Some people (like the old me) like to go into instant angry mode as soon as they even see a donut (cop) driving, let alone are pulled over and confronted by one physically. "Why is this," you ask!? I will give you and answer, and it is this.

Plain and simple, the reason a vast majority of people have Cop Rage is because they heard of, witnessed, or personally been a part of a negative experiences with cop in their life, so therefore they pose more a threat, rather than a figure of safety, so when a person feels threatened, they react with anger…Cop Rage.

Whether the experience is from getting locked up personally by cops, or even just plain out seeing them lock someone one else up that they know, it can leave a permanent negative imprint about cops in their mind, and it can be a permanent imprint. Especially if the situation happens when person is younger, even before you ever started driving.

Example Story: Picture it, when you were eleven years old you and your mom where sitting on the sofa one night watching TV when you dad came home drunk, again, one night and started arguing with your mother. This was not the first time, but this may be the last time, because your mother is pissed off more than usual tonight because she told him last time was the last time. So your mother stands up from the couch and starts yelling at your father and in a verbal dispute, your mother calls your father a stupid drunk, and it really hurt his feelings.

Yes, your father is an emotional drunk. Now, because his feelings were so hurt, your father goes into an emotional uproar and he starts screaming like a manic and he yells at you mom and says, "I am not stupid, but I am sure am mad!", and the he decideds to show her just how mad he is. Your father takes off running like a missile, and then he runs right into the kitchen and then you hear a really big smash. You are your mother run to look into the kitchen and you both quickly see that your crazy drunken father has decided to take his anger out on the kitchen table. You are in shock as you see that you father just smashed the kitchen table with his fists until it broke in half, and now he just tore it in half, literally, and he is now throwing it out the back door. You and your mother scream in shock, and then you watch your father run out the back door and jump off of the deck and land in the back yard. Now the two of you are really worried, and as you both run to the kitchen and look out of the back door, you see your father then run over to the piece of the kitchen table that he just threw outside, and then he picks it up again and then he throws it over the fence and into your neighbor's yard.

Now, your nice neighbors who never bother anybody hear all this commotion, so they look out of their window just in the nick of time to see a half of a kitchen table flying through the air and land in their yard, and then look over into your yard to see a half-naked drunken man outside beating on his chest that is screaming at the top of his lungs. So of course, they called the cops. This is not the first time, nor will it probably be the last time.

It takes not even two minutes for the cops to respond to the call, and as soon as they get to your house they just walk in your front door, because your drunken dad left it open, and they stroll right into your living room where your mother and father are now arguing. Your father at least left the back yard so he could come inside and finish the argument half way civilized, indoors. As soon as the cops show up to your house and they walk inside to see what was going on, your dad turns and sees them, and as soon as he does he immediately decides to pick up the closest weapon, which is a lamp, and then he grabs it and he starts to charge right at the cops so he can try hit them with it physically and push them back out the front door. You dad wants to use the lamp like a battering ram.

The two cops that just entered your house see your dad coming a mile away, as drunk people always move very slow, and then they stopped him dead in his tracks with a punch in the face and then a leg sweep, and then they took him down like a fat sack of potatoes.

As soon as your dad goes down, you and your mother scream and watch in horror and beg for for the cops to stop as you are now witnessing a beating. The cops take your dad down, punch him in the face, put him in an arm bar, then mace him in the eyes because he won't stop moving, and then they hit him in the back of the arm and leg a few times with their clubs, and then they handcuff him and pull him up off of the floor and shake the ever loving S*** out of him. You and your mother scream and cray and you now watch the cops pull your dad outside and then go and throw him into the back of the cop car, while hitting his head on the side of the car on the way in I might add, and then they take him away.

In your mind then, at eleven years old, and still now, at the age of thirty-five, the cops were, and still are the bad guys for doing that to your father, and that is why you have a grudge against all cops and have Cop Rage, you just didn't know it, but now you do.

Now that you are grown up, you still hate cops all and act angrily toward them whenever you are confronted by one because of what happened to you in your past, especially when you get pulled over!

As soon as you are pulled over, I know the first feeling that you get right away, and that is defensive. And the reason why you feel that way is because when you are pulled over, you immediately see the cops as a threat and that there is more of a chance of them doing harm than good, and you also feel as if the cops picked you out of everyone personally, and because of this, you feel singled out, so right away your defensive wall will be put up and you will give the cop a hard time no matter what.

Once you feel this way, just like I used to, that a police officer is a threat and that they will do more harm than good, and when you feel like you are being picked on personally, forget about it, it is all over. Once you have that kind of mentality and thoughts in your head, you are bound to give the cops a hard time when you are approached by them and it is going to end ugly.

So, do you think you have Cop Rage? You don't know, and you want an answer to that age-old question: Do you have Cop Rage!? I am sure you are eager to know now, considering what I told you, and I am eager to tell from what I have learned.

All you have to do to find out is answer some questions that I have put together in a short test Cop Rage Test, one very similar to the "Do You Have Road Rage Test?" It will tell you if you have it, which most do, and if you do, how bad your Cop Rage actually is.

There are two parts to the Cop Rage Test. A **Yes** and **No** part, and a **Multiple-Choice** part, the Yes and No part having forty questions, and the Multiple Choice having ten questions. The way your score yourself is very easy.

For the Yes or No part of the test, if you answer **Yes** give yourself **1 point**, if you answer **No**, give yourself **0 or no** points. For the Multiple-Choice test give yourself **3 points if you answer A, 2 points if you answer B, and 1 point if you answer C.**

If you answer **Yes** to all the questions in the Yes or No part and **A** to all the questions in the **Multiple-Choice** part, you should have a total of 70 points. Once you are done and add up all your points and you can go to the score board and see what it says about your score and how bad it is.

Part 1. Yes and No

1. When you see a cop driving down the road coming the opposite direction from which you are driving, once they pass you do you automatically look in your rearview to see if they are making a U-turn to come and get you (pull you over)?

   Yes   No

2. Do you think that all cops are stereotypical looking? Like they all have buzz cuts, square heads, and fat guts (stomachs)?

   Yes   No

3. When you see a cop flying by in his police car with the lights on do you automatically think they are headed for Dunkin' Donuts?

   Yes   No

4. Have you ever been pulled over by the cops and when they asked you that same question that they always ask everyone: "Do you know why I pulled you over?", Did you ever responded with a, "Yeah because you got nothing better to do!"

   Yes   No

5. Whenever you are driving down the road and see cops sitting at a speed trap, do you instantly get angry and mutter curse words to yourself?

   Yes   No

6. Do you wish you could become a cop just so you could pull them over and give them a taste of their own medicine? Like pull them over and give them a fat ticket!

   Yes   No

7. When you see a cop parked illegally (illegal for us, but legal for them because they can do whatever the hell they want) do you feel domineered and get mad and think about leaving a dirty

note on their windshield?

     Yes   No

8. Have you ever egged a cop car on mischief night when you were younger, or older?

     Yes   No

9. Have you ever spray-painted bad words on the side of a cop car?

     Yes   No

10. Have you ever had to clean those bad words of the cop car during community service that you got for getting caught writing those words?!

     Yes   No

11. Have you ever been pulled over and gotten a ticket? And when the cop gave you the ticket you ripped it up right in front of him!

     Yes   No

12. When you are pulled over by cops and sitting on the side of the road, do you feel like it is one of the most humiliating situations ever?

     Yes   No

13. Do you think that every time you are driving down the road and a cop is driving behind you that he is definitely going to pull you over? And you have to check your rearview a thousand times!

     Yes   No

14. Have you ever been pulled over by the same cop more than once in the same month? And you don't think it was by coincidence!

     Yes   No

25 Do the cops in your town know you or refer to you on a first-name basis?

        Yes   No

26. Do you think the cops in your town have it out for you (they are watching you and looking to set you up) personally?

        Yes   No

27. Do you think all cops were bullies/jocks in high school, and that they are just repeating the process as an adult?

        Yes   No

28. Have you ever been charged with resisting arrest?

        Yes   No

29. Have you ever been charged with assault on an officer?

        Yes   No

30. Have you ever gotten your ass kicked by a cop for mouthing off or being disorderly?

        Yes   No

31. Have you ever gotten your ass kicked by A LOT of cops for mouthing off or being disorderly?

        Yes   No

32. Have you ever been pulled over by the cops, and when the cop was standing next to your car asking you for your license and registration you thought about running over his feet with your car instead and taking off?

        Yes   No

33. Have you ever been in a high speed pursuit or tried to outrun the cops?

        Yes   No

34. Have you ever actually outrun the cops?! We all know that is a one in a million, but I have pulled it off twice.

        Yes   No

35. Have you ever been taken into custody (arrested) and put into the back of a cop car, and when you were in the back of the cop car you tried to kick out the back window?

Yes   No

36. Whenever you pass a speed trap on the road, do you wish you could just floor it and fly past the cop doing 100 miles per hour and give them the finger, rather than slowing down like normal people?

Yes   No

37. Have you ever called a cop a pig to his face?!

Yes   No

38. Have you ever been beaten down and maced for calling a cop a pig to his face!?

Yes   No

39. Do you wish that there were no such things as cops, and that We the People should all be allowed to do whatever the hell we want and be allowed to drive however the hell we want, whenever the hell we want, and however the hell we want to!?

Yes   No

40. Do you wish that there was a special driver's license that you could obtain that would allow you to be able drive like the cops do and not get in trouble by them for it?

Yes   No

41. Have you ever parked in a handicap spot temporarily just to run into a store for a second, and when you came back there was a cop giving you a ticket? And when you see him, then did you verbally assault him for giving you that ticket!

Yes   No

42. Do your friends tell you that it is your mouth that gets you into trouble with the cops?

Yes   No

43. Have you ever been strip searched by the cops?

      Yes   No

44. Have you ever been pulled over and been asked by the cops if they could search your car for illegal drugs and weapons? And when they did you responded with a "No, you can't, I know my rights, you better call my lawyer or you better get a search warrant!" but you really never had a lawyer?

      Yes   No

45. When you are being questioned by cops (for whatever reason) do you tend to get really nervous and stutter your words, even if there is no reason to be nervous?

      Yes   No

46. Have you ever been brought into custody (arrested) for whatever reason and thrown into a holding cell? And when you were in that holding cell you told the cops that if they don't let you out you will kick their A**!

      Yes   No

47. Have you ever thought about becoming a cop for a living, and then you thought to yourself, "Well, I really don't want to be an A** H*** for a living!?" so you never thought about it again?

      Yes   No

48. Are any of your close family cops, like a brother for instance, that you live with? And do you wish to disown them because of their cop attitude is even present at home when they are not on duty! I know, all cops are bossy people.

      Yes   No

Part 2: Multiple Choice

1. You are driving down the road and get pulled over by the cops for speeding. When the cop asks you to see your license and registration, you:

a) curse the cop out for even pulling you over, and you call your mother on the phone to tell her what is going on.

b) huff and puff and give the cop a hard time, and lie through your teeth, making up a bullshit story about why you were speeding and you try to get out of it.

c) treat the cops with respect so you don't get a ticket and you leave with no problems.

2. You are coming out of a store and you see a cop giving you a parking ticket, you:

a) start yelling at the cop that you don't deserves that ticket, and try to rip the ticket out of the cop's hands.

b) try to bullshit the cop by telling him the meter was broke and when he still gives you the ticket you kick your own car right in front of him and let it ruin your day.

c) take your ticket without giving the cop a hard time, and when the cop says, "Have a nice day," like they always do because they have to be polite no matter what…you just say, "Thank you, too, A** ****!"

3. You are driving around town at night when you are pulled over by the cops for looking suspicious. When you are pulled over the cops they ask you if they can search your car, you:

a) tell them absolutely not! You say, "I know my rights and then you can't search my car unless you have a warrant!"

b) call your lawyer on the phone to tell him what is going on.

c) you just let the cops search your car because you got nothing to hide.

4. You are driving home from a friend's house late one night when you are pulled over for a DUI check. When you are pulled over the cops they ask you to step out of your vehicle. When they start to question you, you get loud and defensive and the cop slaps you in the face with his ticket book to shut you up. You:

a) take a swing back at the cop for hitting you in the face like that.

b) get even louder and more pissed off and tell the cop that you want his badge number and you are going to report him to Internal Affairs.

c) shut the hell up.

5. You are driving along when you see a cop block (roadblock) up ahead for seatbelt safety. You:

a) make an illegal U-turn in middle of the street so that you don't even have to pass the cops and you take off at 100 miles per hour.

b) you pretend to put on your seatbelt and pray that when you pass they don't see your out of date inspection sticker.

c) just drive along because you already have your seatbelt on and smile and wave at the cops as they let you pass.

6. Whenever you are standing on the side of the street (for whatever reason) and you see a cop drive by, do you:

a) always think about throwing a rock right at their car.

b) think about giving them the finger.

c) smile and give them a thumbs-up for doing a good job.

7. When cops are called to your house, usually because your neighbors call about a domestic dispute at your house, and when cops arrive, do you:

a) yell at the cops and tell them to get the F*** off your property and if they don't you will kick their ass.

b) argue with the cops verbally but make no physical threats.

c) just stay calm and cool and allow the cops onto your property to explain the situation like a normal person.

8. You are out drinking with a few friends one night when things get a little crazy and you and another person get into a bar fight, over a girl, of course. The fight breaks up quickly and you and a few others are taken outside. When the cops show up to question everyone, you:

a) tell the cops to kiss your ass, you did not start the fight and you ain't telling them nothing.

b) ask the cops if you can at least go back inside and finish your beer.

c) respond to the cops in a proper manner giving them all the information they need and head on home when they let you go.

9. You are driving down the road with your girlfriend when the two of you get into a bad argument. She accuses you of being out with another woman last night and smacks you one in the mouth. You are forced to pull over and get out of the car to continue the argument because you can't do it driving. When you do the cops pull up to see what is going on and you:

a) tell the cops they should mind their own business and keep on going.

b) tell the cops that she is crazy B**** and she need to be arrested for assault.

c) just stay calm and explain the situation to the cops so neither of you get into trouble.

10. You are driving home from work one day when you are involved in a fender bender. An old lady pulls out of a parking lot and you hit into her because you had no time to stop. When the cops show up on the scene to question everyone, you:

a) tell them that they are not needed here, no one was hurt, and they should head back to the donut shop.

b) complain about the time it took them to get to the scene of the accident and if that someone where hurt they would be dead by now.

c) be grateful for them showing up and give them the correct information so they can fill out a proper police report.

Chapter 7: Scoreboard

"Do You Have Cop Rage?" Test Scoreboard

You answer score can range from **70 points**, which is the highest, to **10 points** which is the lowest. The higher the score, number, the worse you are, the lower the better. This is where we see how *Raging* your Cop Rage actually is. Let's see what you got!

70-65. You are one sick, sick puppy! You have such bad Cop Rage that even if Hell Cop from the movie *Highway to Hell* (with Chad Lowe and Kristy Swanson) was driving in his cop car and seen you speeding down the road he would look the other way and hook a U-turn to get away from you rather than try to pull you over.

You have such bad Cop Rage that I bet you are reading this book in you cozy little jail cell that you have to spend at least five years in for your third resisting arrest and assault on an officer.

64-61. The only person in the world who will ever stand a chance at pulling you over is Mad Max himself, from the movie *Mad Max* with Mel Gibson and Angry Anderson. And when Mad Max tried to pull you over I am sure it will be a shootout and a high-speed pursuit, road race to the death, with both of you trying to run each other off the road and shooting you guns at one another.

Gang Bangers (active gang member) like yourself does not take kindly to cops trying to pull you over, and when they do you go all out on their ass.

60-55 How many years' probation did you get for your last resisting arrest and assault on an officer charge? Well, we know that you really did not assault the officers. They just put that down on paper (police report) because you gave them a hard time when they were kicking your ass. You should never give them a hard time when they are giving you a beat down. Fighting back only gets you an assault on an officer charge, everyone knows that. Just getting your ass kicked by the cops and not fighting back will only get you a resisting arrest charge. But you should know that by now!?

Unfortunately, though, with the way you hate cops and how bad your Cop Rage is, you are always going to fight back no matter what because that is just the mentality that you have. It is almost like it is programed inside of you to hate cops. That is how you have always been, and that is how you always will be.

54-51 You have so much Cop Rage and hate cops so much that you can't even watch cops show like *C.S.I.* and *N.Y.P.D. Blue*, because when you see how cops treat people even on a TV show, you get pissed the hell off and want to break the TV.

Why do you get so pissed off? It because it reminds you of what happened to you in your past and how you have been treated by cops before, so it brings up a lot of bad memories for you and you hate it.

In your mind a cop is a public servant (they are) and the last time you walked past a cop you told him to go and get you a glass of water.

50-45. This is how bad your Cop Rage is. Every time you make bacon for breakfast in the morning, you think of the one cop in your town that you hate the most and you start to laugh. Why does it make you smile? Because you like to imagine it is the cop's A** that is burning in the pan!

You also have a picture of this one cop that you hate the most on the dartboard in the basement near your bar that you party at on the weekends.

Just to let you know, that cop also has a picture of you on his dartboard right near his desk and he likes to throw darts at it on his lunch break. What reminds him of you when he is home cooking is when he is gutting fish. Pretty scary, I know.

44-41. Your Cop Rage is so bad that you don't even like to see cops on the road when you are driving, never mind get pulled over by one.

When you go out driving, whenever you see a cop driving around also or sitting at a speed trap, you get angry and upset instantly and mutter curse words to yourself about the cop. You say things to yourself like "Look at this J*** O**, he has nothing better to do but drive around," "Man, I F****** hate cops, all they do is sit and wait to pull people over, jerks."

And forget about when you actually do get pulled over by a cop. When he asks you that same stupid question that he asks everyone, "Do you know why I pulled you over?!" you are the first one to reply and say, "If I get the answer right do I win a F****** prize and/or get to leave!?"

40-35. You Cop rage is mild to moderate and works like this. If you are in a situation where you are confronted by a cop for some reason, say maybe a car accident, and the cop is cool (a person with a good attitude), you will be the same in return.

There is no reason in the world to give someone a hard time if they are not giving you one, but if the cop is a D*** H***, like they usually are, and starts giving you a hard time, you will be the first to do the same in return.

You don't take kindly to being treated like a lesser person, and you will be the first to reprimand anyone that tries to do it to you, cop or no cop. Even if it is from some six-foot-tall, young, in-shape, buzz-cut, square-head, ex-military cop that looks pretty intimidating. He don't intimidate you one bit and you will let him know about it, that is for sure. Especially with the mouth and attitude you got.

34-31. You Cop Rage is not too, too bad, but you are still very confrontational with them and don't like them near your house, let alone in it, or on your property when cops are called to the premises for whatever reason. Usually for a public dispute.

When the cops show up knocking on your door and asking, "What is the trouble?!" you are the first one to reply, "No trouble, as long as you get your A** of my property line, Flat Foot (Cop)!"

30-25. Congratulations, your Cop Rage is not too bad. In fact, you are probably even friends with some of the cops in your town, like the nice ones. Not the Young Punk ones who think who the F*** they are, and they go around bothering and giving people a hard time on purpose.

Like that one young cop jerk who got on The Force (the police force) at the young age of twenty-one because his father was captain and thinks he can bother everyone in town because his head is so big. He has messed with a lot of people, but he has not messed with you yet, the wrong person!

You might also be able to stomach (stand), or actually like, and watch some cops shows on TV. That is not even possible for people who have real Cop Rage. They can't even watch cops on TV without wanting to break it.

24-21. You don't really have and Cop Rage. In fact, you are a good citizen and usually treat cops with respect.

You maybe gave the cops a hard time and got into trouble with them once in your life, and the only reason for that was because you were crazy drunk and angry at someone else and when the cops showed up to calm you down, it did not really work. Trying to calm you down when you are drunk never really works.

20-15. You win. You don't have any Cop Rage at all and you should feel pretty good about that. Having Cop Rage can be a big problem for some people and can get them in a lot of trouble. Trouble is something that no one needs.

When you are confronted by cops you treat them with respect, and are always courteous to them. You may even be a volunteer police officer yourself.

14-10. You don't have any Cop Rage because you probably are a cop and grew up with a cop as your mentor, like your father. You have wanted to become a cop ever since you were a little child, and you followed and stuck with your dreams and they came true. The only way you can have cop rage is if you get mad at yourself.

Chapter 8

How Can I Cure My Cop Rage?

So if you have Cop Rage as bad as I think you do (you scored a 70), there is no cure, no solution for your Cop Rage at all. If you want to live a happy life and stay out of trouble you must avoid cops at all costs, even if it means moving to Africa or Antarctica. Most people, once they have Cop Rage, if bad enough, it will stay that way for the rest of their lives unfortunately. That is just how it is, I am sorry.

Okay, maybe I am over embellishing a little bit, and there may be one way to cure Cop Rage, but I know that most people, pretty much everyone that I have ever known, including myself, are not willing to do it, that is why I did not even want to mention it, but for your sake, the person who is willing to better themselves, I will.

The only cure for Cop Rage is that you would actually have to have some positive experiences with the cops. Yes, you heard me right. You would actually have to leave your house, find a cop, and then have good time with it. You would have to physically try to find or create some situations where you can see cops in a friendly manner and in a positive light for a change.

This is not impossible, and it can be done, but I will tell you that for a person like myself and many other that I know that have had so many bad experiences with cops in their life, they would rather go through some form of torture than to ever do something like this. I know for myself that when I was younger if you asked and gave me the choice between spending a day with a police officer and learn about what they do for a living, or sit in a box with no food, water, or light for a week, I would have picked sit in the box with no food, water, or light for week. And I would have picked that with a smile on my face.

So if you want to cure your Cop Rage there are only a few things that I could suggest where maybe you can get close enough to a cop and have a good experience with one besides getting arrested again and having them laugh at you.

You could possibly enroll yourself in your town's volunteer police program (known as the Auxiliary Police) and go out and work with some cops and get to experience things that they do. This is a drastic measure and not even possible if you have a terrible track record (prior arrests on your police record) like I do. The will not even let you volunteer your time if you have been arrested before.

You can volunteer to do community service and work at your local police department. Yeah, sure, that sounds like fun. Let me go wash some cops' cars that I hate see driving around town, let me clean the floors, put paperwork away, and scrub the toilets of all the men that I despise. All the cops that have arrested me. You must be crazy.

Or you can do an easy one and be nice to a cop for a change. Maybe next time you see a cop hanging out at your local donut shop, maybe you can buy him his coffee and a donut and pay for his meal. That might break the icebreaker between you and cops to make you feel better and relieve some of that Cop Rage! I can see and hear it now, as you turn to look at the cop and yell over to him, "Hey, A** H*** (cough, cough), I mean Officer, can I buy you your coffee today!?"

So unless you are looking to go and make amends to all the cops that you hate and are planning on spending some time with them and changing the way you think about them completely which is almost impossible, I would suggest you do what I do and avoid them forever.

No, I don't mean go incognito and disguise yourself (even though that would help), live under a rock, or move to the middle of the woods of Africa where police don't exist (though I have thought about doing that). I just mean like I said, avoid them at all costs. There are plenty of ways to do it and I will give you some of my best tips that I have that has helped me be free from bumping into cops and getting pulled over from twenty-five times in one year, to now maybe once a year. Talk about a drastic change.

And none of these tips and suggestions are anything extraordinary or hard in any way. It is all just mainly common sense and about being smart, but sometimes we like to forget that we even have these things, common sense and a brain. So read on and hopefully you can find one or more than one suggestion that can help you stay away from cops for a long, long period of time, and hopefully keep you out of trouble, stop you from getting tickets, and most importantly, keep your ass out of jail.

Do Not Break the Law

Most of the times in life I save the best for last, but for some reason in this chapter I want to give the people that don't like to read too much the best one first.

The best thing you can ever do to avoid being confronted by cops is don't break the law! That is, it. There is no secret to it and everyone knows it. People that break the law get arrested, and people that do not break the law, do not get arrested. You get arrested, it is done by cops and that is it. Well, maybe the FBI if you stole some mail, but they are still just cops in a suit.

So do yourself a favor and go out and get a book on laws or look it up online, learn it, and abide by it. Become a good citizen and change your lawbreaking ways, Wild Bill, and let the next guy keep on getting arrested paying fine after fine.

According to the *Rules of the Road* book in California there are thousands of laws pertaining to just the road and driving alone. Not to mention all the laws in your regular everyday life when you are not in your car. There are over one hundred thousand laws that have nothing to do with driving at all.

The majority of us don't spend more than two to three hours a day in a car so when we are not in our car we cut of thousands of laws that we could possible break and get us confronted by the police. So one tip I would give you would tell you donut drive and you avoid a thousand reasons to give a cop to confront you, but that is just about impossible for most people. We all need to drive to get to work and survive in other ways.

So if you do have to drive then learn about the most basic and common laws that apply to driving and the roads in your states so you can avoid breaking them and getting yourself pulled over, or possibly arrested. I know it would be impossible to remember and try to obey them all but you should focus on the main ones.

You know, the main ones like your speed limitations on the road in your state, the rules on ability to turn (New Jersey, there is not left turn, go figure), the limitations on cars that are even legal and allowed to be on the road and pass inspection (you can't drive your dune buggy through New Jersey, either), and know at what age you can drive (some states have different ages).

So for when you are not driving and done obeying those thousand laws and you are pertaining to the rest of your ordinary life, you must obey the other one hundred thousand laws that apply in America. To never break one of those you would probably have to be a saint of some sorts I guess, or be a cop. You know cops almost never get arrested unless the crime that they commit has one hundred witnesses and it hits the local news and it makes it literally impossible to cover up, and even then they don't do time in jail.

To learn all those laws, it would take a lifetime, and to obey all of them you would have to walk around in a bedsheet and change your name to Jesus Christ, and even then you might get confronted by a cop for walking down the street your bedsheet and get a ticket for indecent exposure.

Also, there is one more thing that I did that helped me out more than anything when it came to not breaking the laws and getting arrested. I just tried to obey and focus on all the laws that I used to break and get in trouble for multiple times.

You see, I have had over eight speeding tickets, five careless driving tickets, two reckless driving tickets, four turn on red tickets, and I have gotten at least over thirty seatbelt tickets in my days of driving. I know with this one usually you don't see the cops but I have had to also accumulate over one hundred parking tickets.

So what did I change about my driving. I always wear my seatbelt now, I never speed, I stopped driving in a reckless and careless manor, I never make a turn on a red light (even if I am allowed to and people are behind me beeping at me to go through it), I stopped parking in stupid spots (like on people's lawns and on sidewalks), and I always put money in the meter. Hey, paying two dollars now is a lot nicer now than paying a forty-eight dollars ticket.

Since I have stopped breaking the repeat laws that I was used to breaking over and over again I have avoided getting pulled over and getting confronted by cops drastically. I am a person that holds the record in my town for getting pulled over more times in one year than anybody, over twenty-five times. Since I stopped I maybe get pulled over once a year like a real normal person. My percentage of getting pulled over went down by 90 percent over the last two years. It is a complete miracle if you ask me.

This strategy for not getting confronted by cops on the road also worked in rest of my life. I stopped breaking the laws (committing the crimes) that I was used to doing over and over again and it worked.

I had over six drunken disorderly persons, six noises complaint tickets, two disorderly persons, two simple assaults, two resisting arrests, and two assault on an officer charges. Probably fourteen of my sixteen arrests were in the town that I lived in alone. I saw that judge's face every two weeks for six years straight and I was on and off probation for thirteen years. I don't know how that man still said hello to me with a smile on his face.

So, what did I do, stopped smoking weed, I quit drinking, I stopped fighting with people physically (not so much verbally), and I stopped having parties at my house every weekend (those were the noise complaints), I stopped hanging out in my town (those cops had it out for me), and because I stopped doing all those things I was not confronted by cops anymore; therefore, I avoided getting another assault on an officer and resisting arrest charge and I have not been locked up in quite a while.

If you ask me, I beat that whole vicious cycle that they talk about. That was what I was caught in for a long time. Too bad Wild Bill did not know about my method. If he just stopped shooting people, robbing banks, and gambling, he would have never gotten in trouble. He was what they call "a repeat offender," like me. We like to commit the same crimes over and over again.

So if you have any arrest or crimes that you have committed more than once then I would focus on those most importantly. For the other 99,990 laws that you have not broken yet my best bet for you is do what I do. Use rule of thumb, the Ten Commandments. If you obey by the laws of life in general, then I would say that even if you were as sick as puppy as I was or worse you will be fine in the long run.

Red Sports Car

Do you know why they charge more for car insurance on red sports cars than they do blue minivans? No, not because the cops will notice it first because it is red. That is a plain out urban myth, my friends. Car insurance companies do not take into effect that the color of your car is red when putting together your premium for the year and cops do not pull you over because your car is red either.

It is because the cops and insurance companies know that the sports cars are much more powerful than regular cars, and being that you are a normal person and not a professional racecar driver, you don't have the skills or capability of handling a more powerful vehicle.

Statistic show that most common type of car that are involved in accidents on the road more than any other car, is in fact, red sports cars. Also, the vehicle that has gotten more tickets than any other vehicle on the road is in fact red sports.

Now, there are a few reasons for this. Reason one pertains to the accidents. Like I said, most people think that they can handle the power of a sports car, but in fact, they cannot. I know you think you can handle the 500hp of a brand-new 2010 Red Chevrolet Corvette, but let me tell you this in all seriousness.

Unless you actually have experience on a racetrack with cars of the same amount of power and magnitude that this car is producing, you thought wrong. That baby is a beast and when you unleash all the power of that car on regular streets by putting that gas pedal all the way down to the floor it is like releasing the Kraken (a mythological sea monster). There is no controlling that monster unless you are God or Mario Andretti and it can destroy you and just about everybody around you on the road if you are not careful.

Sports cars put you at a much higher risk for accidents because when you are not capable of handling them, and when you get into accidents guess who are the first to arrive, the cops! That is exactly what cops love to see when the pull up on the scene of an accident. Some young guy in a new red Corvette crashing into people because his ego lost control of the steering wheel and of his vehicle. You want to talk about a cop who is going to give somebody a hard time.

Reason number two pertains to the amount of tickets that red sports cars get. Sports cars, because they are much faster put you at a much higher at risk for getting pulled over for speeding, getting you confronted by cops, and then getting you a ticket. And when you get this speeding ticket or tickets they will make your insurance premium for the year skyrocket. And let me tell you from experience, this is 100ppercent true.

If you get twelve points on your license, and you are allowed twelve before it can be suspended, you will in fact have to pay double on your insurance premium for at least one year, if not more.

If you pay $800 a year for car insurance, you will now be paying $1600. And that is not to mention paying for the tickets that got you the twelve points with to begin with, and then plus the even better part, the surcharges from the DMV (Department of Motor Vehicles) that come along with being a high-risk driver.

And just think about it. How many times have you ever seen a Ferrari (red sports car) cruising down the highways doing 55 miles per hour? They say (considering I have not driven a Ferrari yet, so I cannot say) that being in a Ferrari and doing 95 miles per hour is like being in a regular car and doing 55 miles per hour, same feels. Ferraris don't even break a sweat at 100 miles per hour, and they will do it all day long, where as soon as you and your piece-of-Sh** 1998 Pontiac goes over 65 miles per hour the song "Shake, Rattle, and Roll" by Bill Haley and the Comets automatically comes on the radio, if you know what I mean.

Example Story: Picture it, you are an eighteen-year-old white punk kid, and you just left from a friend's house and you are going to head home, and as soon as you get on the highway you floor it and you start flying down the highway in your little Volkswagen Rabbit. You keep up with traffic, doing 75 miles per hour, but then you push it, even though your car is not supposed to be going that fast, but hey, you see a straight away ahead of you, so you might as well take advantage of it, right, so being that there are no cars in front of you and a mile of open road, you go faster and faster, and amazingly you get your little Sh** box up to 95 miles per hour.

Your engine sounds like it is going to explode, the rev limiter light comes on, and so does the oil pressure light, and as soon as you get up to 99 miles per hour, boom, you pass a speed trap! Perfect timing my friend. You could have not timed that any better.

Right away you see the cop, and he sees you, and you say out loud "F**K!" and then you start to slow down and you look in the rearview mirror to see if he is going to come after you, and of course, he does.

The cop pulls out and then chases you down and pulls you over. You roll down your window and when the cop approaches you, right away he says to you in an angry tone, "You know you were doing about 100 miles per hour back there, buddy!" and then you say, "Sorry, Officer, I really did not notice that I was going that fast, did not feel like it considering this car handles too well!"

BOY, he knows that you are lying straight through your bloody teeth and you just gave him the biggest line of bull S*** that you could possibly give anyone in the world. This excuse only works when you get pulled over and you are driving a Ferrari, Lamborghini, or pretty much any other car that cost over $75,000 and are made by Italians or Germans.

Another reason why so many red sports cars were involved in accidents and traffic volitions throughout the years is because the majority of sports cars are made in red! Think about it, how many times have you even seen a Ferrari in any other color beside red?! Crazy when you think about it. Over 75 percent of the sports cars made in the 1970s and 1980s were red. It lowered in the 1990s to about 60 percent, and now in the new millennium it has lowered even more. About 40 percent of the sports cars made today are made in red. People like options these days.

So all in all, cops do not pull you over and your insurance does not go up because the car is red. It has nothing to do with it. It is because you were speeding and causing accidents in your red sports car that got you confronted by the cops and got you tickets to make your insurance to go up.

And when you think about it yourself you know that color has nothing to do with it. Put a red Corvette right next to a red Toyota Camry. Put a white Mustang next to a white Honda Prelude. Put a yellow Lamborghini next to a yellow Volkswagen Rabbit. It is the look of the car. Not the color.

So if you want to avoid cops and trouble, I would not necessarily say don't get a red sports car, I would just say don't gets a sports car in general. They are much faster than regular cars and that puts you at a much higher risk for accidents and traffic violations, and that is the last thing you want, especially if you have Cop Rage!

If you want some advice, forget about the sports car and get a nice normal car if you want to avoid trouble and cops. You will be less noticeable in blue Toyota Camry then you would be in a blue Mustang. You will be less likely to speed. You will be less likely to get into an accident, and then you will be less likely to get into trouble.

Low Profile

You know why all the mobster and gangsters of today get caught by the cops, because they are all showoffs. Everyone is mobster these days for the attention, for the glory, and actually think of themselves as celebrities rather than gangster. They walk around with flashy women, drive some of the most exotic cars, and walk down the street with money hanging out of their pocket, and they wonder why cops catch onto them and bust them.

It is like in the movie *Goodfellas*. Right after the big robbery that they pull off, The Lufthansa Heist, and Jimmy Conway (played by Robert De Niro) tells everyone that got a piece of the pie (piece of the stolen money) to not to get anything expensive for a while. Yet, what do they all do? They all show up and the Christmas party with new cars for themselves and mink coats and jewelry for their girls. And why does Jimmy Conway get mad and kick everyone the hell out?! Because he knows that the people that are going to notice those nice things first are not the people at the party, it is the cops outside the party!

Cops notice right away when people start flashing huge amounts of money and other materialistic items. Especially if they know you on a personal level like I do. We know you were a high school dropout, got your GED and finished community college by the skin of your teeth and you don't even have a job in the field that you went to school for, now here you are the next day pulling up in a brand-new black Lexus and a getting out in an Armani Suit. Yeah, sure, the EBay stocks that you invested skyrocketed, we all believe that line of Horse S***.

If you don't have the credibility, the paperwork, the college degrees, to be making that kind of money, nine times out of ten we will assume that you are doing crooked (illegal) things to be getting that money, and nine times out of ten we will be right. So if you don't want the attention from cops mainly, stop trying to be an attention hound with you high profile and try to maintain a low profile. What do I mean by maintain a low profile?

Number one, don't walk through the center of your town with gold chains on that could impress Mr. T. and rings that could impress P-Diddy. Keep it covered up until you actually get inside the place that you are going to. Like inside the club, restaurant, casino, because regular people don't want to see your bling, bling (jewelry) buddy, as you walk down the street unless you plan on having the cops confiscate it or you plan on getting robbed for fun.

Number two, dress good, but not too good. You were standing on the corner the other day wearing a FUBU jacket and smoking a blunt and now you got an Armani suit on drinking a glass of champagne. Maybe you can meet me halfway and get like some nice upper-middle-class clothes like Affliction, a regular Armani button-down shirt, some designer jeans, or nice pants? Maybe you can get a nice bottle of Grey Goose Vodka also? That would not attract as much attention if you know what I'm saying, big boy.

And last, now for the car part. You have to maintain a low-profile car if you really do not want to get pulled over and confronted by cops. You do not want to give cops any reason to pinpoint you out from other cars and pull you over. They look for any reason to do so and when you have things like tints (tinted out windows), bigger wheels or chromed-out rims, and things like a louder muffler, that gives the cops every reason to pull you over. You can get a ticket for violation for anyone of those things in a second.

Now, I don't want to say don't buy a nice car because I think everyone has the right to drive a nice car, but you have to be smart about it like most people. Doctors and lawyers also drive around in the nicest BMWs and Lexus's that money can buy, but do you see them with tinted-out windows and a bumping (loud) speaker system that you can hear from five blocks away? Do you!? Doctors and lawyers keep their Beemer's (BMWS) what is called stock. That is what professional people do.

Lawyers don't lift the A** up (raise the rear shocks), put neon light under the car, put racing sticker and stripes down the hood, and go flying down the street with the radio blasting to get everyone's attention. That is what Young Punks, showoffs, want to be gangsters, dumb-A**s like you do to get attention. You are just being a showoff and it gives off the wrong kind of attention/vibe, and no one likes it, especially cops.

So if you don't want to get the wrong kind of attention from cops, never mind regular people, I would say that maybe you should maintain a low profile. Tone it down a bit or be smart about it. There is no reason why you or I cannot have the finer things in life.

But I will tell you this also if you love the high profile and want to keep it without any backlash, move to some place with lots of money where nobody knows you at all, like Beverly Hills, California. Everyone else that is there will be doing the same thing that you are, being flashy, and you can lie your ass off to people and cops saying that you have been rich and flashy you whole life and no one will know the difference and you will blend right in.

Speeding

"What is the number-one moving violation of all time that has gotten more people pulled over and gotten them a big fat ticket than any other moving violation," you ask? The answer to that question, sir, is "Speeding!" This answer not only goes for the number moving violation of all time in America, but just about every country in the world also! Who would have ever guessed it? Speeding is the number one offender of the road.

Well, it is true that any time a cop sees you doing just one mile over the speed limit, just 26 miles per hour, it gives that A** H*** the right to pull you over and give you a ticket, but usually cops will not pull you over and mess with you if you are doing just 1mph over, that is unless that have it out for you personally which I am sure if you are reading this, they just might. Cops usually do not mess with people unless they are going at least 5 miles per hour to 8 miles per hour over the speed limit. Then cops start to pull people over and question them.

There are a million reasons in this world why people might speed, but I will throw out there just a few of the top reasons just for fun and just to inform you a little bit of why most do, and why maybe you are doing so, and it will enlighten you a little bit.

Number one, and for the most part which is true, people don't even realize that they are speeding. People tell that to the cops all the time when they get pulled over and usually the cops don't believe them, but it is true. Who has time to look at their speedometer when they have their kids jumping around in the back seat of the car, they are looking at their watch, and they are talking on the cell phone because they are pressed for time and are trying to make it to little Johnnie's birthday party on time? If they looked at the speedometer they might actually crash because it would take up what is left of their brain power.

But for real, people don't realize how easy it is to go over the speed limit and not notice. Especially when we are traveling alone. That is one of the biggest factors when it comes to forgetting about speed. How many times have you been driving down the road alone and just thinking about something else and just keeping up with traffic, and next thing you know you look at your speedometer and you are doing about 85 miles per hour? If you are keeping up with others that are speeding, you will forget to look at your speed and you will assume everyone else is going the normal rate of speed.

Also when you are traveling alone, there is no one there to tell you to slow down and remind you if we are going too fast. Certain people, like your wife, will notice as soon as you take a turn to sharp and she will get on your case about it and tell you not to doing it again. Certain people are there in life to remind us of certain things, and when they are not there, we forget.

Number two, you have to speed. Sometimes there are emergencies, or sometimes there are normal reasons for us to be speeding. Like when you are driving down the highway for instance. Sometimes you have to speed up faster than other moving cars traveling along with you so you can pass them and or get out of their way in time so as get off at and exit and not to cause an accident, yet when you get pulled over and you tell the cops, "I had to speed up," they don't seem to grasp that concept. I always wanted to tell a cop, "Hey, listen here, dumb ass, if everyone traveled down the road at the exact same rate of speed, 55 miles per hour, we would all be stuck, you catch my drift, Officer Stupid, now go learn some mathematics!" Sometimes speeding up CAN, in fact, prevent an accident, but people don't seem to believe that one.

Number three, you are pressed for time. This is one of the most crucial factors of speeding that gets people into Road Rage altercations, gets people into accidents, and gets people pulled the hell over for driving like Dale Earnhardt Jr. The major problem is not only being you speeding, but when you are pressed for time you stress yourself the hell out, and when that happens how do you act? Irrational, crazy, stupid, you can't focus, and you shake, and you are doing all of this in a speeding car! Not a very healthy combination and it kinda sounds like a recipe for disaster if you ask me.

People always think that they will save some time by speeding, but the risk that you take by doing so, and usually for such stupid reason like "I am late for work again!" is so idiotic and dangerous that you can't even imagine. You put your life, and worse yet, others' lives in jeopardy all because you want to get to work in ten minutes, and it is a thirty-minute ride. Not too smart. Take your time. If you are late for work one more time this week it should not matter anyhow, they know how you are by now. You are always late on Fridays.

Number four, you just like to speed. Some people just like to speed even if they do know the all the consequences that speeding potentially has. Tickets, accidents, and possibly death. They like traveling at a higher rate of speed then everyone else, they like the feel of passing people on the road, they like to get to their destinations quicker, and they also like the adrenaline rush that speeding gives them. Plain and simple, some people just like it, like myself.

So there are many more reasons why people could be speeding, but who cares. That is not what this is about. What I want to tell you about is the ways you can avoid speeding, or if you are going to, what to look out for and how not to get caught and pulled over by the cops so you don't have to get your eighth speeding ticket and your second disorderly people's ticket for yelling at a cop. This is about trying to avoid cops completely, remember.

Here are eight good tips that I got for you that you could try if you want to avoid getting pulled over for speeding....

Number one, never speed downhill! Don't you know by now that cops always sit at the bottom hill waiting for people to come flying down it? If you are going to speed, speed uphill, that is if your car can handle it. Some cars don't have enough pep (horse power) to go faster up hills, kinda like your old Ford Taurus.

Cops know that people like to fly down hills so that they can save on gas. They do it all the time, and if you don't hit the brakes you will get plenty of momentum and be able to travel for at least a mile without hitting the gas pedal. I did it the other day. Only thing is you have got to go over 55 miles per hour to really have this work out in your favor.

And you know what it odd, you would that that because we are trying to all good people we want to save the environment (gas money) you figure cops would give us a break on this case, but guess again, Joe.

Number two, never speed at the end of the month. That is quota time! Quota time is the end of the month when cops must meet the amount of money for the month that they must bring in through traffic violations and other citations. Yes, they must bring in a certain amount of money a month for a combined total that is known as the quota. And if all the cops have been slacking on giving out tickets throughout the month, they will make up for it and meet the quota and make it happen in those last few days.

Even though most people say that having a quota is illegal and they do not even exist, I beg to differ and have heard different. There is one saying that cops go by: "A ticket a day keep the sergeant away!"

Number three, if you are going to speed, know the area! Know where the cops sit and hide out at (speed trap behind billboard) or hang out at (Dunkin' Donuts). Like for instance the town that you grew up in. You knew where all the cops hide out were, just like they knew where all of yours were. You knew how to avoid them at all times.

When you speed through an area that you don't know, you put yourself at much higher risk for getting pulled over because you don't know when you could possibly pass a cop that is parked at a speed trap or just hanging out. When you know where they might be hiding or hanging out at you won't take that chance of flying by them doing 22 miles per hour over the speed limit, that is unless you are going around and looking for trouble like I used to.

When you know where the cops might be hiding, you take yourself out of risk for getting pulled over because you won't speed past that area, or you can avoid it completely.

Plus, one of the worst things when you get caught for speeding and get a ticket for it in an area that you don't know, like two hours away down the beach, is not necessarily the ticket at the time that you get that sucks, but it is if you decide to fight the ticket in court and have to drive two hours back to whatever town it is in to do so.

It is not like going to court in your town that is right there. It is a nightmare. So do yourself a favor and if you want to avoid this, don't speed when you are out driving outside of your town at all in fact. It will make life much easier, trust me.

Number four, the rule of thumb behind speed traps. The trick is to not only know where they might be hiding but also when they might be hiding!

I know that in my town they would switch shifts at midnight so there would never be a cop sitting in one of the traps at that time. That is the time when my friends and I would make the move with beer from one friend's house to another when we were under age.

Number five, know where cops can hide out legally. I know that cops cannot sit and hide out on private property legally. Like they can't park their ugly cop car in the driveway of a privately owned houses, stores, or pieces of land and set up a speed trap. They can't do that legally. Cops can only sit on property that is owned by the government. Like places such as post offices, local parks, VFW and AMVETS buildings, schools, and basically anywhere on the street or highways. It is just that when cops sit on the street you can see them stick out like a sore thumb from a mile away. That is why cops always try to find places to hide, but they have to be legal about it themselves also, or when they pull you over you can say to them, "Hey, listen, Officer, you can't pull me over, this is entrapment!" but most likely he will give you the ticket anyway unfortunately and you will have to fight it in court.

Number six, stay in the middle of the pack. When you are speeding along and traveling down the highway with a pack of other cars that are doing the same, do this, try to stay in the middle of all of them.

Concept goes like this. If you are the first in the pack, you will be the first to get hit with his radar gun when you pass a speed trap. If you are the last person in the pack, you will be the first A** that he pulls up behind if he decides that he wants to pull someone over that was traveling along in this pack of speeding cars.

Think of it as like a cougar that is chasing a pack of zebras. You know one of the poor guys on the outside is going to be the first to get hit with those might claws and teeth.

Number seven, get a radar detector or laser jammer. That is right my friends, they sell all types of device that blocks/counter acts the actual cop's radar gun that they used to try to catch you when you are flying down the road. Radar detectors give you notice when a cops radar gun is in the area (like when you are driving near a speed trap), and most importantly, it block/stops the cop's radar gun from actually getting a read out on your speed when you fly past him.

Radar detectors and laser jammers are legal in almost all states in America to own and use. You just have to check with you state code and limitations against them. Like in Utah, for instance, you may own a radar detector legally, but not a laser jammer.

Also, just to let you know, radar detectors and laser jammers are completely illegal to use on any military property at all. So if you plan on driving through Fort Dix any time soon, I suggest you leave the thing at home unless you want to get arrested by an MP (Military Police). And you thought the cops in your town were bad, just wait until this guy's chews you out for messing around on his territory.

Number eight, play the game of follow the leader. If you are going to speed down the highway, do it behind the guy who is going faster than you. It is like sending the fat kid out on the ice first.

You can drive slowly for a while until you see someone who is speeding along and going significantly faster than everyone else and then you get behind them and tail him for a while. Just stay a safe distance behind them, maybe ten cars' length, so when the person speeding in front of you does pass a cop at a speed trap, you will see them hit their breaks and you will have more than enough time to slow down yourself so the cop doesn't see you speeding behind them.

Number nine, the added bonus, put up a picture of a loved one. This is in one of the earlier chapters and also and also helps with Road Rage. If you speed a lot and it is a problem, and you always have to look at your speedometer to know how fast you are going, put a picture of someone that you love right near your speedometer so that you can see it every time you look at it.

Usually when we are speeding down the road and we look at the speedometer we say things to ourselves in our head like "Well, I am not going that fast," "Maybe I should slow down," and then you continue to speed anyway.

What the picture will do for you is change what you say to yourself in your head. Next time you are speeding and look down at the speedometer and notice the picture instead it will make you say in your head, "I have to stop speeding!" The picture of you loved one, child, wife, brother, dog, or whoever it might be, will remind you that you have loved ones that you need to make it home to, and that speeding is one way that you might not make it home to them.

Speeding puts you in danger for tickets, more tickets, accidents, and worst of all, possible death. The higher the rate of speed that the car is traveling, the greater the chances are for casualties when being involved in that accident and that is a proven fact. If you want a better chance of making it home to your loved ones healthy and in once piece, you have a much better chance of doing so when you dive slowly.

Speeding is not a joke and it should not be done at all unless it is an absolute emergency and there are no other options. Speeding should be left for the racetrack and not for the everyday roads where people can be hurt because of it. Avoid speeding, avoid tickets, avoid accidents, and avoid the cops!

Maintain Your Car

Not only do really nice cars, sports cars, exotic cars, big trucks, pimped-out cars, tricked-out cars, stick out like a sore thumb and get noticed by cops first on the road, but so do the really, really S**** ones. It is a shame, but they don't fit in with the normal cars on the road, and driving a beat-up car will just get you pulled over and laughed at by the cops, and then ticketed for everything that is wrong with the car.

Example Story: Picture it, you are a fifty-seven-year-old white man, and there you are driving down the road in your 1987 Dodge Aries K car and you are coming home from your girlfriend's house one night. As you do so, you listen to some relaxing music, you drive at a normal rate of speed, and as you cruise on down the road heading home and enjoying your ride, you suddenly pass a cop sitting at a speed trap. You look over and see the cop sitting there, and after you pass the cop you then look in your rearview to see if he is going to pull out, and of course the cop does so, and then he starts to speed up to get behind you, and then he follows you for a minute before he decides to pull you over.

While the cop is following you, you then ask yourself in your head, "I wonder why this cop is following me and is he going to pull me over?" "I was not speeding when I passed him," "I am not drunk so I am definitely not swerving!" "I wonder what is the matter."

The cop after finally following you for a few blocks turns on his lights and pulls you over. The officer walks up to your car and you roll down the window. The officer greats you and you great him, saying hello. After the formal and kindly greeting, then officer asks you, "Can I please see you license, registration, and insurance, sir?"

You respond, "Why certainly, Officer," in a shaky, girlish voice and then nervously lean over and dig through you junk filled glove compartment looking for the paperwork with things falling out of it (hopefully not your weed). So the cop stands there and waits patiently until you finally get all the paperwork together. You hand the officer all the papers and then he asks you another question. He asks you that famously stupid question that all cops ask everyone:"So, do you know why I pulled you over?!"

You respond with "No, sir, I don't," and put a dumb look on your face, because you really don't! Like I said, you did nothing wrong.

After you say that, the cop then leans over, looks at you in eyes, raises his fist, and then he swings his arm and he punches you in the arm and he screams out as loud as he can, "PADIDDLE!" You gasp because you are in shock that you were just punched first of all, and the you grab your arm because he actually hit you pretty hard and you are in pain. Then you look at the cop and say, "What in the Sam Hell was that for!?", and then the cop laughs at you and says in in return, "I pulled you over because you had one headlight out!"

Padiddle is a game that is played amongst youngsters, and sometimes adults, when they are driving around town in your friends' car and smoking weed, and whoever is the first one to spot a vehicle traveling with one headlight, tail light, or brake light out and yells padiddle when they see it, and then punches the person/ persons closest to them in the arm, and then they win a padiddle point. Whoever has the most padiddle points at the end of the road trip wins.

Cops can spot a nice car from a mile away, but they can hear and smell a crappy car from two miles away. You have to maintain your car brother. If you cannot afford to keep up on it, seriously, junk it or give it away.

Junk cars that have broken tail lights, burnt-out headlights, dents, broken windshields, loud mufflers, out-of-date inspection stickers, leaks oil, have squeaky breaks, burn oil, and have a spray can paint job with bumper stickers all over it will only be a money pit for you. Trust me on this one.

Cars that are like this will only get you pulled over again and again and again, and then you will never have the money to fix the car because now you will need to the money to pay all the fines that you got because of the car. It is the absolute truth.

Cops hate to see shit boxes (beat-up cars) on the road and they always pull them over and give them violations. They are just tickets waiting to happen.

If you have a car like this, and I had many like this, get rid of it. It will only get you pulled over and confronted by cops and it will give them the opportunity to harass you, make fun of you, and give you tickets also, and that is the last thing that you want to have happen to you if you have Cop Rage. You do not want to be put in the predicament because it gives you motive to lash back (retaliate verbally) and if you do that to the cops, you might get pulled out of that beat-up car and then get beat up yourself and arrested.

Cops always pull over beat-up cars not only because they are noticeable, but because they can be potentially dangerous also.

If you are driving with broken lights no one will see you and can cause an accident. If you have a cracked windshield in can cave in on you and kill you. If your car leaks or burns oil it will destroy the environment (we already have enough global warming). If you have squeaky breaks or burnout brake pads they can break and you can get into an accident. If your car has a bad paint job and bumper stickers it is just an eyesore.

And also, when you are driving such a junky car, a lot of the time cops pull you over not because they want to bother you, some cops actually do understand that you dot make that much money and a beat-up car is all you have, but they have to make sure they you can actually afford the insurance on it. Lots of times when people are driving these beat-up cars around, and can't afford to fix them, they most likely can't afford insurance either, and it is the truth.

Not all cops want pull you over and bother you because you drive a 1976 Ford Bronco with bald tires, a broken exhaust, a cracked windshield, and give you a ticket. They just want to make sure it is insured because God forbid that things does decide to lose it breaks or blow out a bald tire and hurt somebody, at least it is cover by your Geico Insurance! So do yourself a favor, junk the old duster and walk, ride the bike, take a bus, or car pool and do the right thing. Try to save up until you can buy a car that is half decent (anything over five thousand dollars) and swallow your pride for now and do what you have to do, and it will all work out for you in the long run. It always does.

Out of Sight, Out of Mind

So I hope this chapter has helped you and given you some insight on how to avoid cops, that is if you need to as bad as I do. If you have a bad case of the Cop Rage, then you want to keep your distance from cops as much as possible if you want to stay out of trouble, and keep out of trouble.

Road Rage Buddha says, the farther you drive away from trouble, the closer you get to safety.

Chapter 9

What Do I Do if I Am Confronted by Cops?

Chapter 8 was solely based on how to avoid the cops and how to try to stay away from them completely. Whether it be avoid passing speed traps, driving a different car, or just plain out not breaking the law, in the last chapter I tried to give some of the most efficient ways and tactics to not get into trouble by the cops and keep from Cop Raging. Like they say, "Out of sight, out of mind," or in your case, "Out of sight, out of jail!" If you don't see and talk to the cops, you won't end up in jail.

Why is that, you say? Because you know that every time you get confronted by a cop, your Cop Rage acts up, you get agitated, and then you open up your big mouth and say something stupid, and then that gets your ass kicked by the cops and then you land in the drunk tank (holding cell) again for the night. That is just how you are, just like your father, and that is probably how will be for the rest of your life. I am sorry to say.

But this chapter, Chapter 9, is based on what to do if you actually are comforted by the cops. Like for instance, if you are pulled over again (for the third time in one month), I want to tell you what not to say, and what not to do to the officers that you are confronted by so you don't get your ass a third ticket, or worse, get dragged out of the car and beat up again for talking smack (talking trash) to the cops.

In this chapter I am giving you a bunch of ways on how to stay out of trouble, how to not let your Cop Rage act up, and I and I am letting you know what to say what not to do/ say if you are confronted by the police again, God forbid.

So yes, it is true that some people, hopefully yourself after you read this chapter, can still have Cop Rage pretty badly and yet (such as you and me), when they are confronted by the cops they do not actually have to flip out every single time and get beat and thrown in jail. They know how to keep their composure in front of the cops, even though they don't like them.

So, I am going to teach you how to keep your composure when you are confronted by the police, and there are bunch of easy ways to do this and I am going to name a few of the top ones that have helped me. And I hope you can use yourself in the future and they help keep you out of trouble, because one thing that we all know is that you definitely do not need any more trouble with the cops. One more violation of probation mister and you are going to jail for five flat (five years with no parole).

Don't Be a Wise A**

One thing nobody likes in this world, especially the cops, is a little wise A** that likes to go around thinking they are tough, and cool, and acting like they are better and smatter then everyone else. Especially the type of wise ass who acts cocky also, those are the worst. Last thing we need in this world in another Joe Pesci wannabe.

The wise-ass cocky people that I am talking about are usually the type of people that end up being lead singers in some shitty band, and they don't even sign autographs for the little people because they are too good for that, and they think that their music is actually good and they have talent, when they really do not.

Example Story: Picture it, so you are out on tour with your shitty little band, The Mud Dogs, and driving from Washington State to New York City when your tour bus (spray-painted school bus) is pulled over by the State Police (the real cops), as you are going down the highway.

So the cops, State Police, pull you tour bus over and when they approach the bus ask if everyone can step out of the vehicle so they can see all the passengers. You immediately get agitated because you feel that there is no need for this and that your rights are being violated. You think you know it all with you little attitude so you start mouthing off to the cops as soon as you step out of the bus.

This is you. Hey, "There is no need for this, what is going on here, we are not doing anything illegal so we don't have to do anything you guys ask, now who is in charge here and I want some answers!?" So the cops just ignore your stupid little attitude, and then they decide to sit everyone down on the side of the road (all the passengers that were in your bus), and start to search the bus.

Two cops search the tour bus (spray-painted school bus), and two other cops stand guard and watch you and your friends sitting on the ground to make sure that no one does anything while they search the bus.

As the cops search the bus, your wise A** attitude gets worse and now you start mouthing off as you are sitting on the ground. You say, "How long is this going to take, I got to be to New York City and put on a show in twelve hours, do you know who I am, I am the lead singer of The Mud Dogs and you cops are going to catch hell for this!"

The cops pay no mind to you at all because hey, they have dealt with your kind many times, and because they are the only humans that don't kiss you're a** unlike you little roadies, so you get even more upset now because your big Ego is hurt. You keep mouthing off, and because you get no response and you want to get your message across, you decide to stand up without the cops asking you to do so because you want to go and talk to them. Bad move, buddy, because as you stand up the two cops that were watching you and your buddies on the curb jump on top of you, take out your legs, slam your face on the ground, almost twist your arm almost out of socket in the process, and then they put you in handcuffs.

That is what you get for having a wise-aA** attitude and stepping out of line leader of the Mud Dogs. You have to remember this. The cops don't care who you are, where you are going, what you are doing, or if you do or don't know your rights! Cops do what they want, when they want, how they want, and that is that, and you should just shut up and let them do their job because if you step out of line when they are doing it, you are going to catch a hell. Most people don't want to hear this though, that cops are allowed to use physical restraint when a person does not comply with a police officer's simple requests.

By you stepping out of line and not doing what you were told, and because you were being a wise ass only makes them doing their job much more difficult for them, and then in turn it only comes back on you. And when they give you a cop a hard time, they will always give you a way worse one then you could ever give to them buddy. Kind of like how the cops made you look like a Mud Dog for real by slamming your face in the dirt.

And just to let you know something, one thing that you said to the cops that you wise A**, or should I say dumb A** lead them onto, was when the cops showed up you immediately said, "We are not doing anything illegal!" As soon as you say that, the cops will automatically know that you're a** is up to no good. People who are at fault and get caught red handed, the first thing they say is, "What, I wasn't doing anything wrong!"

So you should have toned it down with that wise A** attitude and you should have just chilled out and waited until the cops said something to you, but you were too eager to get your message across and you wanted to throw your power around that you thought you had Mister Mud Dog. Now guess what ?! Now the cops are taking you to jail, and only you, and they charging you with the marijuana that they found in your tour bus, and only you, and they are letting everyone else go. How do you feel about that?

And just to let you know, that is why the State Police pulled you over in the first place. Because you tour bus looked like it was on fire driving down the road with all the pot smoke pouring out of the windows!

So unless you want someone to put you in your place one day, whether it be a regular person or the cops, Joe Pesci, I would suggest dropping the Wise A** attitude and stop throwing Ego fits and just chill, because if not, it will only result in you getting your ass kicked by someone who really is a bad A** and it could cause you a lot of trouble. Unless you got the credibility, the muscle, the attitude, and the power to back up being a Wise A** (like Chuck Zito can), it would be a good idea to cut it out.

Do Not Overreact

One thing you never want to do in front of the cops if they do decide to show up, especially considering the cops always love to show up at the wrong time like they always do when things are already at their worst in a situation, is overreact! No one likes to experience drama, nor do they want to be in a heated or a confrontational situation when it can be avoided, and that especially goes for the cops.

What, do you think cops like to show up at your house when you are drunkenly fighting with your mother and father, or pull you over when you are fighting with your girlfriend in the car and swerving all over the road. Do you think they do that to you on purpose? I used to. I know, cops always know when to show up, and it is at the wrong time, if you catch my drift.

Cops already know very well that once they get in the middle of heated situations such as when loved ones are fighting and the drama and the intensity is high, that the heat (the fault, negative energy, yelling) is going to get put right onto them as soon as they show up, and it always does. Cops know it, they are well aware of it, and they are trained to handle it. It is actually part of their job as a police officer to stop these intense situations, such as domestic disputes filled with drama and hatred, and to keep them from escalating and getting any worse, so as no one gets hurt. The cops are there as so you are your parents don't end up trying to choke one another to death if the fight if it keeps escalating.

Example Story: Picture it, you and your girlfriend are home in your studio apartment the other night when you start having a heated discussion about what you two might eat for dinner. You both say, "There is never anything to eat here!" She blames you for eating all the food, and then you blame her for not doing the food shopping properly, never doing the dishes, and then also for not doing your laundry, like she is supposed to because she is a woman?!

Not a smart move buddy, because she was already in a pissy mode and now that you made that demoralizing feminine comment to her about her supposed to be doing your laundry because she is a woman, you really hit the trigger. Next thing you know the heated discussion about dinner now turns into a full on fight that is blown out of proportion, and the result is the two of you end up throwing pots and pans at each other, and bringing up resentment that you have against each other from the last four years of being together. Your girlfriend brings up the time that you slept with her sister, and you bring up the time she crashed your car. Crazy how much we hold onto, I know. I use to live by that old slogan also, I forgive, but I don't forget.

You both flip out while screaming and yelling at each other and you break each other's stuff for over twenty minutes, and then just like last time, and but of course, the cops show up. Your poor neighbors called them on you again.

So as soon as the cops show up, they start knocking (or banging) on the door. As soon as you hear the door you jump and then you fly to the door like Superman and open it and as soon as you do you start yelling at the cops as soon as you seen them and you scream out, "Help me, Officer, help me, I have a crazy woman living here with me, please!"

Your girlfriend comes running over with your favorite shirt and starts then she starts to cut it up with a scissors right in front of you and the police. You run over and try to rip it out of her hands and stop her and then you look at the cops with a sour look on you face and say start, "You see, Officers, this B**** is crazy, help, help me!"

So the cop's kind of listen to you, and then they come into the apartment, stop the two of you from fighting physically, and then they handcuff the both of you and lock you up for a domestic dispute. They take you both down to the station for a few hours and processed (fingerprint, paperwork, then give you a court date) the both of you and then give you a court date. Yes, the two of you will have to go before a judge and explain yourself and probably pay a heavy fine because like I said, this is not the first time either.

Wonder why that happened? Maybe it was because the both of you were overreacting right in front of the cops? Cops are not marriage counselors and they don't care who was at fault before they showed up or who did what when. All they know is what they are seeing right now and that is you and your girlfriend are fighting physically!

There should be no reason for any situation to escalate to that level in their eyes, and especially not in front of their eyes! They know that next thing would have been either you trying to hurt her physically to get your shirt back, or her trying to stab you with the scissors for being a jerk and sleeping with her sister.

When the cops showed up you should have both stopped what you were doing and tried to calm down. Overreacting to them, or in front of them about anything is just not a smart idea. When cops show up to where you are, no matter what is going on you have to keep a level head and not overreact. If cops see you acting crazy, they will just assume that you are crazy, and they will place you under arrest, or at least handcuff you until you calm down and they can assess the situation at hand. You have to remain calm not matter what situation you are in that cops might show up at and get involved in.

Example Story: Picture it, you are driving through a parking lot one day after food shopping when you are involved in a little fender bender in the parking lot. You were pulling out of a parking spot when someone driving by hit your rear end. You get out of the car and then wait for the cops to show up.

When the Cops do show up to make sure everyone is okay and to make a police report about the accident, you then get back out of your car and then walk over to the cop and start yelling and overreacting and saying, "It is the other jerks fault this happened, they pulled out in front of me, and you should lock them up!" Now wise my friend. You are yelling, you are blaming people, and worse yet, you are telling the cop what he should do in the situation and you are telling him how to do his job. That is beyond over reacting buddy. Yea, we all get pissed off when we get into an accident, but no, not everyone gets out of their car and yells at the cops for it.

That is way overreacting! You will only get yourself into trouble and the cop will probably give you a ticket and blame it on your for overreacting like that, mainly because you were telling him how to do his job. Cops hate that.

Never overreact when cops are around. Always maintain a level head and normal tone of voice and you will be alright. You will look like a normal person, and those are the type of people you want to be like if you want to stay out of trouble.

Limit Your Time around Cops

If you are put in a situation where cops do show up, if you somehow can, if at all possible, limit your time in that situation and make it as short and as sweet as possible.

If I know you, and I am sure that I do, if your Cop Rage is bad enough, the longer you stick around, the more of a chance you have of opening your mouth and getting into trouble!

Example Story: It is your best friend's twenty-fourth birthday and you and a few friends show up at the local watering hole (bar) to celebrate. It is you, the birthday boy who is your best friend, and another five or your buddies that show up to this gathering of good times. You all start to pound down (chug, guzzle) some drinks, talk and laugh about old times, and have a good time celebrating.

Everyone has a good time for a while but then birthday boy gets upset for some reason. You can see and angry look on his face so you go over to him to ask him what is wrong. He does not say because he is so mad, but then you notice for yourself what is going on because he keeps on looking a certain way.

As you look to where your best friend is starring, you can now clearly see what he is mad at as you see his ex-girlfriend that he broke up with a week ago standing on the other side of the bar. And guess what, she decided to show up at the bar with a walk in with her new guy, and that is yours and birthday boy's ex-best friend! You guys use to be friends with this dude. Birthday boy gets madder than a bull when he sees a red cloth, and you hope that he will not doing anything about the situation and just let it go because you don't need any more trouble, but he does because he is not the type to let things go.

So now you cringe as you see birthday boy walk right over to his ex-girlfriend and then he starts yelling in her face. As soon as he starts yelling, then his other ex-best friend, her new guy, comes over and tries to say something to birthday boy. Ex-best friend says, "Hey, can't we talk about this like men?" to birthday boy, and then birthday boy says, "No!" and then he swings his fist right past the girl and he punches his ex-buddy square in the eye.

Birthday boy and his ex-best friend start to wrestle around and fight in the bar. You are the one who sees what happens first and run over to birthday boy and try to stop him from fighting. You try to pry the two men apart and you almost get hurt in the process. A few other people jump in now to help you break the two men apart, and then you hold birthday boy back. He does continue to jump and yell and brigade his ex-best friend and ex-girlfriend with a massive amount of curse words and terroristic threats verbally as you continue to hold him back.

Of course someone calls the cops like they always do. It is like people have 911 on speed dial or something so the cops show up within no more than two minutes, and by this time the fight has been broken up but everyone is still inside the bar yelling and screaming. The cops walk into the bar and of course they approach you and birthday boy and then start to ask what happened.

As soon as this happens if you are ever in this predicament, do yourself a favor and don't say anything! The more you say you saw, the more the cops will want to question you about the whole ordeal that took place, and that will keep you there for a much, much longer then you need to be. You want to leave this situation as soon as possible.

Let birthday boy answer the questions for himself. Even if you did see what happened, play the blind mouse game: "I did not see anything,

Officer." If you do say that you saw exactly what happened they will want to put you in the police report as a witness, and then they might even want you to go down to the police station with birthday boy and answer more question if they need it.

If birthday boy is going to get locked up for fighting it is his fault and you don't need to go down to the police station with him to prove that you are his friend. In fact, you can help him more by not getting involved and going your local bails bondman so you can bail him out if you have to.

Also, if everyone says that they do not know what happened exactly, just the two guys fought, then the cops will not even be able to make a real police report if everyone keeps quiet. They will only be able to charge the two men for fighting and that is it. No one else has to be involved and they will be let go.

You want to limit being a part of any crime scene as much as possible and that will help you limit your time in some situations such as this one.

Also you could have done two things. You could have tried to drag your buddy out of the bar before the cops showed up and ran. Then you would have not had to deal with cops at all. Or you could have just left yourself and not partaken in the situation at all. You almost got hurt by trying to break up the fight, and you had to get confronted by the cops and put in a situation where you could have almost been hurt and arrested.

I know you want to say, "Well, he is my buddy and he would fight or get arrested for me." Yes, I believe this very much so and feel this way myself and would never leave someone in a fight either but you have to take this into consideration also.

Other people (normal people that don't fight or get arrested) have always said this to me: "Well, a real friend would not have put you in a situation where you have to fight or get arrested."

So next time the cops show up, be quite and try to get out of there as fast as possible, even if it means leaving people in the dust, this is your A** that is on the line. You know how you are and you don't need to be in any situation that involves cops at all. It will only result in you getting into trouble and that is the last thing that you need.

And on one last note, choose your friends wisely.

Only Speak when Spoken To

Well, we know that you feel Cop Rage on the inside, but the only way to let it out really and let people know how you are feeling on the inside, is letting it out through that big mouth of yours. So the last thing you want to do when you have that Cop Rage feeling moving around on the inside is speak. If you speak when you are feeling Cops Rage you will only say something stupid, really stupid, aggressive, or violent, and then it will get you into trouble.

So one of the best ways of avoiding saying something stupid or wrong to cops when you are confronted by them is limit your speaking also. This mean only speaks when spoken to! Unless the cop asks you a question, and you are answering it, you should not be saying anything. Keep your mouth F****** shut and I mean it buddy!

And when they actually do ask you questions you should not only answer them quickly, but answer them in as short of a manner as possible also. I am talking about single-syllable answers, my man. YES, or freaking NO, and that is it. The more you talk, mumble, and argue with the cops, and babble on about something stupid the more you are going to piss them off, and the more of a chance you got at get arrested.

Example Story: You are out with a few friends one night at the local bar eating some food and having a good time. Everyone is having some drink except you because you have work in the morning and you are a responsible adult, yeah right. You do stay kind of late, though, and leave around midnight.

As you walk out of the bar and get into your car to leave a cop drives by you. You kind of see him, and he kind of sees you. As you get into your car and pull away, after about driving only one mile, guess who comes up behind you to pull you over, the cop that just seen you walk out of the bar. I wonder why he is pulling you over.

So the cop follows you for a while and then finally puts on his lights and tells you to "pull over" on his loud speaker, and he does that whole embarrassing and annoying part that they do.

You hear him clear as day, and his light blind the hell out of you, so you pull over. The cop walks up to your car and asks you for your license, registration, and insurance. Your response is "Yes sir, Officer," which is proper. So you go through your glove compartment and as soon as you have your paper work you hand it to the officer.

After that he asks you another question. He asks, "So where are you coming from tonight and where are you going?" You go into full on detail about what you did and say, "Well, I went to work today, then to my girlfriend's house after work, after that I went home and did some cleaning, and tonight I went to the bar to meet my friends who were all drinking and taking shots but I did not because I have work in the morning, and now I have to get gas and then go home!"

You're a dumb A**, for real. All you should have said was "I am coming from seeing a friend, and I am going home!" and that is it. Keep the answer short and sweet, honey. He does not want to hear your whole story, and when you do tell him, you give him opportunity to believe you did something, and then you give him reasoning to ask you other questions.

Now you gave him reason to believe you are out drinking and driving. You told the cop that you were in a bar, and all your friends were drinking, but you did not drink

Yeah, I bet he will believe that one. That is like saying, "I went into a Chinese man's house, I wore my shoes, I watched the Chinese man cook some Chinese food, but I did not eat any of it and I put my shoes on and I left." Why would you do that? Anyone that goes into a bar drinks, anyone that goes into a Chinese man's home eats Chinese food. Especially if you told the cop that you were with your friend and they were drinking. You should have just said, "I just dropped someone off at the bar," or, "I stopped by to see if my friend needed a ride home, but they were not there." It sounds more realistic, and you will not leave a door open for the cop to assume you were drinking, so he will not ask any further question.

Plus, now, that you pretty much gave him reason to believe you were drinking by practically admitting it, he will now ask you kindly to step out of your vehicle so he can give you a DUI test, you will get defensive and start and argument with the cop because you feel like you are being mistreated because you really were not drinking and it sucks and I know because it has happened to me and just about everyone that I know.

When you are confronted by cops, for whatever reason, you want to keep the answers as short as possible. Yes, or no, and if they ask you for details, like "Where were you on the night of June 18, 1994?" you say, "Home!"

Not that I was here, then I was there, and then I went home. You have to get one story and stick to it. One story, one answer, one outcome.

The less you talk, the shorter the answer, and plus the smarter the answer, the better off you will be in the long run my friend, so trust me on this. Like the old saying goes, the less people know, the better off they are, so this should go for the police in your case if they ever ask you any questions.

Be Apologetic

No, saying you are "sorry" does not mean that you are admitting to guilt or being a sissy. It just means that you are being polite and apologetic and showing concern for the situation at hand, even if you did or did not do it.

If you are confronted by the police, for whatever reason, whether guilty or not, hopefully not guilty, say that you are sorry as many times as you can without actually annoying the cops.

Example Story: You are a 40-year-old white man that works as an attorney, and it is a Friday and you are going to be leaving work late because you have a ton of paperwork left over from the week to do. So 6:30 rolls around and you finally finish all your paper work, so you finally get to leave work late and angry, and did I say really angry because you ate once all day, and we all know how cranky you can be when you don't eat. You can only imagine how bad this is going to be.

So in your state of anger you get into your car, start it up, pull out of the driveway, and then start to drive home. You are ok for about five minutes into the ride, and then your anger kicks because you are getting even hungrier now, so then you start to fly down the road angrily. Yes, you start Road Raging because you are angry it doing so makes you feel better, and you also think you will make it home faster by doing 100mph and cutting everyone off that gets in front of you. Yea, many of us Road Ragers think and act this way when we are angry and hungry. So, in your speeding Road Rage escapade to try to get home quicker to eat, you start weaving in and out of traffic like a snake and you give everyone that tries to slow you down the finger, and when you are almost half way home a cop witnesses your Road Raging escapade.

A cop driving not too far behind that it getting onto the highway going your way you see you up ahead and witnesses you cut someone off so he decides to pull you over. He chases you down and he has to cut a few people off himself to catch up with you because you are going extremely fast. You have not noticed him yet, so you have not let off the gas pedal! As soon as the cop catches up to you he puts in his sirens and then he pulls you over. You are in shock as soon as you hear the sirens, and you pretty much know that you are screwed if the cops seen you giving people the finger.

So, being that you are sick now and you just lost you appetite, you pull over and roll down the window and await your death sentence. The cop then walks up to your car and asks you for your license, registration, and insurance. You get it together and then hand it to him. Then the officers ask you that famous question: "So do you know why I pulled you over?" like if you get the answer right you will win new car or something.

You respond with a "No, sir, I don't," and play the part of Dummy Dwarf and put a stupid look and your face. The officer then decides to tell you what he saw and why he pulled you over because you sure as hell don't seem to know, so he says, "Well, I saw you driving a little fast and seen you cut someone off back there and nearly cause an accident."

Next, you give and even dumber response and you say, "Well, the other guy would not let me in, I had no choice but to cut him off!" The cop looks at you like the dumb A** that you are for saying something so stupid, and then you say something even more stupid. You ask the cop, "So why am I getting pulled over, for almost causing an accident?" Man, you are dumb. And you are an attorney you said? What kind? An Intellectual Property Lawyer because you sure as hell aren't a criminal one.

When the cop told you why he pulled you over all you would have had to say was this: "Geez, Officer, I am so sorry, when I went over into the other lane I did not realize the other person was so close to me, I am sorry," "I would never cut someone off, and I am sorry if I was going fast, I was just trying to merge quickly so I would not hit the divider or the person in front of me!"

Number one, the cop will be able to find out if you are telling the truth or not by looking at your driving record. He can do that right from the front seat of his car on his super computer, but for the most part, if the cop sees that you are genuine and are actually sorry about what you did and you don't really seem like you are the type of jerk that does this on the road normally, as you do every day, A** H***, he might actually let you off the hook (let you go with a warning).

Cops hate when people try to lie, and especially when they do it badly, and don't admit at all to what they did and the driver tries to play the cop for the fool (treat the cops like he is dumb and he did not see what he saw).

You see, in your apology, you say that you did do something, and that what the cop seen was correct, and you did not mean to do it, so you do not admit to guilt.

If you try to say that you did not do it all, and the cop actually seen it, you are 110-percent going to get that ticket. Cops hate that. The cop seen it with his own two eyes, and now you are telling him that you did not do it. Basically, you are calling him a liar to his face, and that is a plain out insult.

Or, if you do what you did also and then try to blame someone else for what you did wrong, such as cut someone off and then blame it on another driver. If that other driver was no pulled over also, trust me, then cop will not go and find them no matter how much of the incident was their fault because he has you, and only you, so you are the only one that you should be speaking for and trying to get out of this mess. Not blame it on someone else.

So next time you are confronted by the cops, for whatever reason, make sure you say you are sorry. Even if you don't damn well mean it, just act like you do. Like Elton John song says, "Sorry Seems to Be the Hardest Word." Nobody likes to say it, but in the end, when you do say it, it is for the better of you, not the other person.

Don't Feel Special

A lot of the times, actually and probably every time, we are confronted by the cops, for whatever reason, right away we feel like the cop picked us out of everyone else to bother, like we are that special.

You feel like the cop decided to pull just you over out of the other one hundred thousand cars speeding down the road and give you a ticket. You feel like the cop decided to walk up to just you in the crowd at the Ozzy Osbourne concert and bust you for smoking weed (marijuana). You feel like the cop decided to stop just you and take your beer away for drinking in public in Times Square on New Year's Eve. You feel like the cops got called to just your house out of all the other million houses in America. Mind you, all of those things I mentioned happened to me.

Like the cop had it out for just you, only you, and no one else in the crowd. Like it was something personal. If you believe that, you will automatically go into Cop Rage every time you are confronted by a police. You have to wipe that belief right out of your head or you will be in for trouble every time you are confronted by the police, whether it be pulled over, or on foot.

It is kind like that one specific cop in your town that you think has it out for you because he pulls you over at least once every four weeks. You feel like he pulls just you over and never does it to anyone else. Like he has it out for you and only you. If you believe that you probably also believe that the policed department hired him and put him on the payroll just so he can keep an eye on you. The hired this specific cop to handle and keep an eye on just you! Don't think like that.

Don't feel special. You are just not there (at work with him) when he pulls over the other two hundred people all day long for his eight- to ten-hour shift a day, nonstop without lunch. Cops do what they do to you, once every couple of weeks (that is how often you seem to get in trouble with the police), to other people all day, every day. It is not just you! You are not that special, trust me.

So do yourself a favor and wipe that belief out of your head and you wont be so agitated next time you get confronted by the cops. And if they do keep on picking you out of the crowd for some reason it is prob- ably because you are sticking out like a sore thumb or doing something stupid to get noticed. Cops don't want to keep approaching you, you may be doing something that is making that happen.

Be Polite No Matter What

If you are confronted by the cops, God forbid, be polite no matter what! Listen, I know you hate sucking up to people and being nice to them just as much as everyone else in this world does, but fake it if you have to. Nobody cares if you fake being nice and no one will know differ- ence, especially if you are good at it like everyone else at your job. What, you think your coworkers are nice to you and all the other cus- tomers that come to the counter all day long for real! Sorry, my friend, they are all acting and faking it.

Most people in life are as rude and as crude as possible and they will go through most of their lives like that, living off of what is known as dry sarcasm (kind of like a dry drunk).

So just like when you are at work, pretending to be nice to people, like all coworkers do to the customers, do the same thing with cops. Just pretend to be nice. Even if you have to clench your teeth until they bleed and lift up your cheeks with a forklift, put on a fake a smile and say thank you, just do it.

You also can think about it like this. When you are confronted by a police officer he is only doing his job. He is actually at work. So guess what, he is probably just pretending to be nice to you as well. What, do you really think that smile of his and good cop attitude is real? Especially after dealing with so many negative people and vibes like he has to all day long. Cops actually have to be polite to a certain degree. They can't just go around yelling, cursing, and pushing people around, 'cause if they did they could get in trouble and lose their jobs. Just because they are cops does not give them the right to go pushing people around.

I know being polite to someone you hate so much is tough, like the police, but think of it like this. It is only for a short period of time that you have to be nice to them for. Maybe ten minutes if you get pulled over, maybe twenty minutes if they come by your house for a noise complaint, maybe just one night in a holding cell if you get locked up for fighting. It is only for a short amount of time, and it will work out better for you if you are. The meaner and angrier you act toward police, the same they will do to you in return, hence, you get more tickets, or a worse beat down.

Plus, like I said, it is only for a short period of time. You can act nice at work for 8 hours a day so you don't argue or fight with anyone. And you acted nice for seven months to your old roommate until that last day when they finally moved the hell out and you blew up on them (told them how angry you have been about everything). If you can do it there I know you can do it here.

Be nice and remember, what you give out in life, is what you get in return.

Last but Not Least

If you are ticketed or arrested, for whatever reason, you have to remember, it is not the end of the world! Well, as long as you have money to pay a good lawyer!

That is the beautiful thing about this country, America. No matter what the case may be (O.J. Simpson Case) you are innocent until proven guilty. Other countries it is the other way around. Your A** is guilty until proven innocent, imagine that one.

You stand a chance to fight almost anything in court and win, unless you admit your guilt. That is the most solid form of evidence that any court can ever have, is your word. As long as you say I did not do it, until you go to trail and the jury decides that you did DO IT, then you did not do it.

You can plead not guilty to any ticket (moving violation) that there is, and you can plead not guilty to any crime, and you can take it to court and you can fight it out! So if you do decide to plead not guilty and fight it out in court, you can defend yourself (not a wise choice), or you can hire an attorney to defend you (wise choice). You can go to court with you lawyer, you can bring evidence of what happened between you and the officer that day if there was a dispute, and you can tell it to a judge and a jury. And guess what, there is a chance that you might win because not every single thing that cops do to people are right. They can pull people over wrongfully, and they can give them wrongful tickets. And I hope in your case, that that is true, that you were punished wrongfully. It has happened to me, and I won two of my cases in court.

I hope this chapter helped my friends, and if you ever do go to court because you decide to fight it out with the law, just remember what Road Rage Buddha says: Always dress to impress!

Chapter 10

My Story

This is a True Story my friends, not on Example one this time: From the first day that my first set of wheels wherever put on the road, I believed that owned that baby. Just like that song "King of the Road" by Roger Miller. Whether I was driving my Big Wheels (Bigfoot edition) as a child, my bicycle as a kid, my moped, my mini bike, my motorcycle, or finally my first vehicle which was a truck that I got when I was eighteen, I have always driven with Road Rage. In fact, now that I think about it and look back, I may have had Road Rage since the day I was born?! I came out speeding and yelled at the doctor, "Get out of my way, slowpoke, I need some booby!"

Maybe it is another gene to look for in people in the future, the Explosive Road Rage gene? Or maybe that is what the Big Bang was? Two gods having Road Rage. Two immense entities of power bumped into each other driving across the vast and infinite road ways of the universe and they yelled at each other, they got angry, got into a fit of Road Rage, they fought each other with their mighty powers, and once their mighty powers collided, "Boom!" thus we were made. Hey, you never know. Nobody knows the real answer.

Since the first day that I was put behind a moving vehicle that I could control and drive I have driven fast and furiously (no pun intended). To me it was always just more fun this way. I have always had a thirst for the *ROAD*, a hunger for the race, and stomach full of *RAGE* to win that road race.

I have always hated to lose and I guess I have always use rage to help me win. Whether we are talking about playing board games, video games, card games, or even thumb wrestling as a kid, I have never liked to lose, nor did I even want to ever be second in second place if there was more than one competitor in that challaneg. In the words of the great Dale Earnhardt, **"Second place is just the first-place loser!"** and I could not agree more, Dale.

I can remember my dad yelling at me when I was driving my Power Wheels (three-wheeler edition) in the back yard and the ripe age of just four, and he walk out the back door and come out on the porch and then he would point at me and would scream out, "SLOW DOWN KID! You are going to get hurt, or hurt your sister!" and then he would repeat this over and over again, but I never listened, and when he went back inside then I would ram into my sister on purpose with my little three wheeler, and I would push into her bike and throw her right off the con-crete slab and send her flying into the muddy dirt on the side of the above ground pool. She was going to slow around the bend on her bi-cycle so I had to do something about it. We only had a 20-foot-by-20-foot slab of concrete to go in circles around in the backyard (we were too young for the front of the house), so when she went too slow either I had to cut her off or push her out of my way. That is just the way it was. Go slow, get cut off! And I never felt bad about it or thought twice, even at that young age of 4. Mind you, my sister was mentally handi-capped (slow), and I still had no remorse on her. This coming from a four-year-old kid. You can only guess how it progressed as I got older.

Then into my younger teenage years it was racing with friends on bicycles or Rupp mini bikes (those funny-looking things with snow blower engines) around town for fun. When we were racing I always had to be first in line. "Slow down!" my friends would yell at me as I passed them going Mach 5 on my mini bike. All my friends had three-horsepower engines on their mini bikes but I had to have the faster mini bike of course. I had a five-horsepower engine on my mini bike with no governor. That means my friends could do about 30 miles per hour on their mini bikes and I could do about 50 miles per hour on mine. "Eat my dust!" I would yell to them as I would pass them on one wheel.

"Slow down!" the pedestrians walking through the park would yell at me as I came flying by nearly running them over on my mini bike and making them jump from the walking/bicycle path, that I turned into a racetrack.

I would go through the park and take the turn faster and faster every day, trying to see how fast I could go from one end of the park to the other end. My friends and even other kids that we did not even know would sit there and time me and watch like spectators as I flew through that park like Richard Petty at Daytona 500. Finally, one day I did end up crashing. I lost it in turn three, went off the racetrack (or pedestrian/ bicyclist path), and hit a puddle of mud and flew for about ten feet. I nearly broke a rib, and hurt my knee pretty good but I got right back on my horse on rode ride after that.

But to tell you the truth, there was excitement in crashing to of course. "Crash and burn!" I used to say all the time since I saw that movie *Robot Jox* as a kid. Great movie. I always wished I could just fly around in one of those big robots instead of driving in a car and if someone messed with me (cut me off or beeped the horn at me) I could just shoot a laser at them and destroy them. I always thought this would make my life much easier. Yes, I always thought crazy things like that.

And even when it came to bicycles as a kid I always had to have the fastest BMX bike (Elf Zr1, best BMX of 1994) and I always had to be first one in line when we were riding in packs. I would race anybody, anytime, and anywhere. We would ride our bikes around town for hours on end every day during the summer. Day in and day out. This was the days before computers, so we would get bored after playing Nintendo after an hour and then we would spend the next eleven hours on our bikes. I was always the one doing crazy stunts also, such as trying to grab onto the side of cars to go faster, fly down the biggest hills in town, hitting the biggest jumps, and of course, riding my bike through traffic and messing with cars on purpose.

Funny story about riding bikes when we were kids. This one time my best friend and I started racing down a dirt road on our bicycles, as we cutting through a park in the town that we lived in and cutting across an old gravel road near the train tracks to get home faster. In the beginning of the race, my friend got the jump on me (a head start) so he was a head of me for a while in the race home across this old gravel road and I did not like that at all! I got very angry and used that Rage within to make my bike go faster and I started to catch right up to him.

Mind you, I had on my bike at the time, a loud speaker that I had bought at Bradlees for like ten dollars. It was kind of like one of those things cops used to yell at you with when you are protesting, just a mini cheap one. There was the horn that was mounted in the handle bars, a wire, and also the intercom in which you could speak through. I took the intercom off my handlebars as I was trying to pass him and then I pressed the button and I stated yelling at him with it and saying, "I am going to pass your fat A** so move the F*** out of my way!" and when I was just on the verge of passing him, I then raised my hand because I was actually going to hit him in the back with intercom and my hand so I could try to slow him down so I could win the race! Yes, I would do dirty thing like that to win also.

Too bad things did not turn out that way. I caught up to him and as I was flying right beside him and I tried to hit him with speaker, as soon as I raised my hand and tried to hit him, the speaker that was mounted on my handle bars fell off and it went right between the front spokes of my bicycle. I am sure you can image what happened as my bike had turned into an instant catapult! I had passed him alright, just flying through the air. When I landed, I skidded for about ten feet on my stomach in the gravel and broken glass and got cut up pretty bad. Served me right, but did I learn my lesson, hell no!

A few years later when I became a teenager I got a moped, and boy did I used to love to speed around town on that sucker. I had a 1981 General 5-star and boy was it fast. I would fly around and cause a scene and try to race people everywhere I went. I fixed it up to make it go faster of course, just as any young Road or Speed Demon would do. I put on a bigger motor and a bi-turbo exhaust pipe on it. I would try to racecars, other mopeds/motorcycles, and any just about any object that moved really. It was street legal, and yes, I was pulled over on it a few times. One officer that pulled me over gave me a ticket for speeding and said the usual, "You better slow down!" he said. "I seen you doing about 45 miles per hour back there and you were in a 25-mile-per-hour zone!" I just kind of laughed it off as usual and went on my way.

Funny thing is though, a few hours later I was speeding on my moped again and I came flying around a turn off a side road onto the main road in town, and as I came speeding around the turn and nearly crashed right into the same cop that just pulled me over earlier and gave me the ticket. You should have seen the look on his face though, it was priceless! He looked confused, angry, and shocked all at once. After I flew past him he put on his lights and then he started chasing me right away. I turned off of the main road and then drove through the park and hoped right onto a path in the woods and I took off. He chased me through the park but I lost him of course as soon as I got on that dirt path and headed for the woods. Four-wheels can't go where two-wheels can. I ditched him down the dirt roads, but I sure as hell heard him yelling at me over that loud speaker and telling me to come back, and if I don't that he will catch me anyway. Needless to say I laid very low for a while and did not use the moped much after that because I did not want to get caught.

And then even when I was driving on my motorcycle that I got a year later, as I had a motorcycle before I had a car, I would Road Rage and I was very dangerous and crazy. I drove around popping wheelies, cutting through cars when I was driving through traffic, and I loved jumping things. I had in my mind also that when I was on my motorcycle and driving through traffic that I always had the right of way. "Me first!" I would yell at other drivers, "I am on a motorcycle here and you have to yield to me!" I when I would drive down the highway I always tried to get my motorcycle to go as fast as it could go also. My buddy and I use to race our bikes down a long stretch of road near the Meadows in Lyndhurst NJ that was only a 35mph zone, but I think we both he speeds well over 100mph when we use to drag race down that strip.

"There is no other speed to drive but full speed!" I used to say to my friends. Every time I got on the highway with my motorcycle I was driving full speed. If a car tried to slow me down or even came near me out came the leg, boom, and I would kick their car. I guess I should have tried to join that biker gang from *Mad Max* the movie (the first one), or maybe the Hell's Angels would have accepted me as a prospect because of how crazy I was!

But even after all the road racing and Road Raging I did that would make you think that I was just a danger when driving a vehicle, as it turned out, I was also a danger on foot!

One more funny story for you, as a few friends and I were coming out of a club at 3 A.M. in New York City one night. We were all hungry so we went to a sandwich shop around the corner from the club to grab something to eat, and get our food to go. After we got our food, we were all walking back to the car with it. As me and my friend were walking back to the car side by side, not in any Gay way, we then looked at each other kind of funny like, not in any Gay was, and the next thing you know we both just started running and racing to the car for Shotgun (front passenger seat in a car) and we did it without even saying a word to each other. Usually, someone yells "Shotgun!" first, but this was a sneak attack on both our parts. He was a head of me as we were racing and he was just about ready to win as we were only about 100 feet from the car and I knew I was not going to be able to beat him so I got upset (here comes the Road Rage) and I tripped his ass. I kicked the back of his foot so that it would hit his leg, and when I did it, it worked like a charm and then he went down like a sack of potatoes! Man, you should have seen it, it was funny as hell. There he was on the ground, all messed up and cover in Taylor Ham (known as pork roll to the states other than New Jersey) egg, and cheese. I felt bad and offered to buy him another sandwich but he was pissed off and refused. It was all good, though, because I won the race.

So finally, after all those wonderful moments growing up as a kid and a teenager, the Road Raging maniac that I was, was finally about to be put behind the wheel of his own car for the first time as I was turning. I can remember that glorious moment when it finally came. I felt as if I had waited to drive and own my own car my whole life.

Something that I felt I was born to do! I literally felt as if I was made to drive a car since the day I was born. I literally started asking my father if I could drive his car when I was only eight years old. My father, being the cool guys that he was, actually let me and then he put me on his knee and let me drive that 1976, straight 6, cherry red, four-door Chevy Nova that he had around in Bradlees parking lot one night. It was the coolest thing and it was embedded in my brain as pure happiness and glory, and I knew that I would only have this feeling again when I would have my own car, and that was about to come.

I was now old enough to drive, and all that craziness got put behind the wheel of his own automobile! Talk about scary. I bought my first vehicle at the age of eighteen. It was a medium sized truck, of course. Hey, it was either that or a Ford Mustang and my father knew that I was definitely way too crazy to get one of those, so I got a nice Ford Bronco II (one of the smaller ones), and it was something that I saved up myself to buy and I called it "The Tumbler." Remember, you always have to name your car or truck.

I remember thinking to myself on that wonderful day that I will never forget when I turned 18. I got in my truck, sat behind the wheel, then grabbed and said, "They have laid this beautiful black pavement just for me and no one should bother to hold me up on the road or get in my way, for if they do, I shall Road Rage upon them a Road Rage that they have never seen the likings of." I come up with this one, *"If there is no rest for the wicked, then let me never make a pit stop!"*

I started my truck, pulled out of the driveway, and I made pulled away and I made a scene wherever I went from that day forward. I drove all over town. I would cut through the parks (something only the cops can do). I would race on the main roads in town. I would drive on people's lawns and peeling out (like schools and neighbors) who pissed me off. When we would go off-roading, I would always try to jump things. And I also loved messing with pedestrians (throwing things and yelling at them and so forth).

I also used to get chased by cops often, and I did try to outrun them but I did get caught most of them time considering my Bronco was fast, but not that fast. I guess I thought I was just like Burt Reynolds from that movie *Smokey and the Bandit*. I used to say to myself, "Man, if I had Bandit's car I would have never have gotten caught!"

But out of all the crazy thing I loved to do when I would go driving around was my was that I really liked messing around with other cars, or drivers, especially. It was as if everyone was an opponent, or someone to mess with in my eyes.

I would head out to the highways at night, sometimes with a friend or other times alone, and I would literally go looking for races and people to mess with on the road on purpose. Hell, I had nothing better to do. I did plumbing by day and nothing but drive around and bust balls (bother people) by night. I am Italian, what else is there to do besides bother people when you are bored?

The first people I would mess with on the road were people who were driving too slow, and guess what, when you are driving everywhere at 95 miles per hour pretty much everyone else is driving slow! So I had to mess with everyone. I could not be behind someone for more than two seconds without flipping out and yelling at them and Road Raging. I would then pass them and yell to them, "Get off the road, you slowpoke, and learn how to drive you A** H***!"

For those first couple of years that I drove, there was literally not a night that I did not go out and find someone to race with, and if I could not find someone to race with, I would try to provoke and agitate someone who was not even driving slow or bothering me the point to where they would eventually race me. If I did not pull up at a high school with my buddy and try to find some other Young Punks to race us for money, we would just go and drive around town and provoke normal people that we did not even know into racing with us, and trust me, we knew all the tactics how to provoke a normal person into racing with us, or least piss them off to the point where they would Road Rage at us. It was fun to me.

When I would win races and get into these crazy Road Rage altercations, after a while I started bragging about it. I guess it made me feel a sense of accomplished in some weird manor. Like my pride was at a high for the day! Another victory of racing on the road or another crazy Road Rage altercation story with me fighting that I could tell to all my friends about and make them laugh. Another story to gloat about. Another person taken out in a fit of Rad Rage. Another stamp on the side of the truck. Kind of like what the Red Baron (that German pilot from WWII that killed more people than everyone else) does when he would shoot the enemy down and put a stamp on the side of his plane. I always wanted that stamp, just in car or truck formation of course instead of a plain and put it on the side of my vehicle.

But when I would lose a race, and this did not happen often, even if I did have shit box (a beat-up car). Hey, my friends did not call me, "The Ghetto Mario Andretti" for nothing. If I lost it would bother me for weeks! I could not even sleep at times if I lost a race. That is not one thing I am good at like a said earlier, losing.

But after years of driving like a maniac, though, things got way out of hand. What I once used to do as fun, Road Rage and race with people and being funny and busting people's balls when I was younger did tend to get more serious as I got older and became more like a sickness as the years when on.

The Road Rage had gotten way too serious and it was causing way too many problems in my life. It was kind of like a drinking problem that escalated. That is the only way to explain it. What once was fun, was fun no longer and it was now causing me hell, yet I still kept on doing because I really did not know there was a problem to tell you the truth!

It was like I was addicted to Road Rage at one point. Like I stated earlier, I don't think that there was not one single day in the whole year of 2002 that I did not get into a Road Rage altercation. Every day that I got into my car, or even other people's cars, I had to yell at somebody, race with somebody, curs at somebody, or throw something at somebody from my car. It was every day!

It was so much of a problem that I almost lost two jobs because of the way I drove also. I did construction for some years and I had my own company van. Though my first boss practically owned the town that our company was based out of and had the cops so they say "In his back pocket," if you know what I mean, so I was never worried about getting pulled over when I was driving the van around. I could drive around town and do 50 miles per hour through a 25-mile-per-hour zone down the main road in town and the cops would not bother me one bit, but I tell you who would though, the local people sure would!

People used to call my boss on me all the time and say to him, yelling over the phone, "Hello, hello, I just seen one of your vans flying down my street doing 50 miles per hour!" My boss after getting that same call for the second time, had already confronted me about this before and said, "One more call, and I am going to give it to you buddy," and I got that call, of course.

This was him that third time he got that complaint over the phone about me driving like an animal through town: "WHAT THE F***, you are driving around town in a Goddamn billboard you dumb Ass****! If someone calls here one more time I am not going to fire you! I AM GOING TO STRANGLE YOU!"

There was smoke coming out of his ears and his eyes were bright red! I just kind of laughed it off after he left. I was still very childish. I always thought it was funny also when people would get that mad at me, such as my father, or any other adult for that matter. I know it was for a good reason but I did not want hear it at the time. I worked there for about another year and luckily no one else called in on me but I still drove like an animal, of course. I had not learned my lesson yet.

This crazy, obscene and destructive behavior went on for years and years. Just about from the age of eighteen to twenty-four. Crazy reckless driving, Road Raging, and racing people wherever I went. Getting pulled over, getting tickets, in and out of court rooms, and losing my license many times. I also went on to destroy eight cars in about five years.

I always had to ask my dad to help me fix my cars after I broke them and it was the worst because there was always an argument. Thank God he was a mechanic! After my dad looked at the car and he diagnosed it as destroyed or totaled, I would then just go out and buy another junk box to beat on. I never bought a new car because I knew that I was just going to destroy it anyway. That was just the nature of my mentality and behavior at the time, sad to say. I would rather destroy a 1,000-dollar car than a 15,000-dollar car. Why kill an investment. At one point I had beaten up so many cars that I was literally like a junkyard at my house. I had six cars broken-down cars in the yard and I was walking to work. I had managed to run all my cars into the ground and lose my license again. Talk about crazy.

I got into many Road Rage altercations over the years also, leading to fights (verbal and physical), accidents (my fault and not my fault), tickets upon tickets (always my fault), and eventually just becoming dangerous and never learning my lesson.

But in my mind at the time, I was young, crazy, bit of a heavy drinker, and I liked to fight with people (physically or verbally), and I basically thought that this behavior was normal (normal if you were like Cole, played by Tom Cruise in *Days of Thunder*). But this was how I grew up, crazy! With fighting in my house hold that I grew up in day in and day out. I had a crazy father with a combative personality who used to love to argue every day, though he never did Road Rage, and a nutcase for a grandfather, who always Road Raged! My grandfather was the first one in his town in Italy to ever even own a car! You can only imagine why his Road Rage was so bad.

They were both car mechanics and you should have seen those two when they used to work on cars together, the fighting would last the hole time they were working on the darn thing. Fighting for hours on end. It would not stop the whole time. They would throw wrenches at each other, curse, flip out, end up walking away, and then coming back and doing it all over again. Kind of like the meaning of insanity. Doing the same thing over and over again and expecting a different result! Yes, these were then men I looked up to, insane, and therefore I ended up the same way, insane. I was just like them, fighting, cursing, driving like a maniac, fighting with people at work, drinking alcohol heavily (wait— they never did that?), and doing the same thing all the time, yet expecting a different result.

So it was not until years later, after I lost my license for the fourth time, after walking to work for six months just to pay back all my surcharges and fines to get my license back, and after all my friends and family would not even get into the car with me anymore to even accept a ride anywhere, and then I questioned myself. I asked myself, "What the hell is wrong with me and why won't people drive with me anymore?" I was asking myself this question for some time before a friend made me realize that it was a Road Rage problem.

Here came the awakening. A friend and I were driving to the mall one day when I began to Road Raged at someone. Typical, I know. The reason for my Rad Rage was because the guy who was driving in front of was driving way to slow, so a cut around him, drove in the wrong side of the road, and when I passed him I beeped my horn at him and I yelled at him and I told him how he should learn how to drive, mind you, I was driving on the wrong side of the road and speeding.

After I did that the friend who was with me asked me a question. He asked "Do you have to Road Rage every time I am in the damn car with you man!?" I responded with a "No, no, no, they are holding me up, they make me Road Rage, it is them, not me!" Then my friend said to me, "Man, you have a serious Road Rage problem, buddy, and it is you, not them!" This was something that no one had ever said to me before, and I guess he had said it at the right moment in my life because it actually made me think. Then my buddy also said to me, which is real and funny, "you are going to kill someone or us if you keep driving like that, and if I die in a car, I want to die in a Ferrari, not a piece of junk Ford Bronco." I laughed of course, but he was right.

It was like telling an alcoholic that he has a drinking problem, yet they don't see it until this point. The alcoholic wonders why his life is in shambles from drinking, they get locked up, they pay the courts, they fight every day, they lose their jobs and their loved one, and then then wonder why is drinking not fun anymore, and why is this happening to me (and only me), and it everything is everyone else's fault, so they still continue to do it, drink.

It was just like me. I had way too many tickets, I still had court pending, I was still yelling and fighting with people on the road every day, Road Rage was not fun anymore, and I was wondering why is this happening to me (and only me), and why is everyone else always making me Road Rage, and yet I would still do it, Road Rage. That was my main problem, I was blaming everyone else for my Road Rage. It was like I was living in denial of Road Rage.

So I asked myself, "Do I really have Road Rage?!" I took a look at myself and some problems that I had.

No one would even get into my car with me anymore, not even if they had to go to the hospital. My father actually said, "NO!" to me when I offered him a ride to the hospital one time after he cut his finger.

He said, "I would like to make it there in one piece, so I'll drive myself, thank you."

My father would rather drive to the hospital with one hand, then take a ride from me. He cut his finger open very badly and would risk his life driving with only one hand and on painkillers then to even get into my car and drive with me. That tells you something right there. If not, then how about this.

All my friends and family were afraid to even let me sit in their car, never mind let me drive their car, as that was completely out of the question!

Also, I had eventually destroyed and fixed so many cars that my father once told me that "I will not fix another car for you no matter what, not even if that was the last car on earth!"

My girlfriend at the time would not even let me drive anywhere at all when we were together, not even to blockbuster that was down the street.

So eventually after I cracked up eight cars in six years. When I had gotten pulled over nearly fifty times in five years, and I hold the record for getting pulled over more times in my town in one year than anyone else! After I had my license revoked for having too many points on it over four times. After paying nearly $355 a month just for just liability insurance on a 1984 car in the year 2004. After I had walked (or rode your bike) to work to many times at the age of twenty-four. After I had almost died in three major car accidents and one major motorcycle accident.

The S*** finally hit the fan, and then one day I finally said to myself, "WOW, maybe I do have a problem?!" No S***, Sherlock.

So, I asked myself, "What can I possibly do to help myself with this Road Rage problem!?" And it just so happened that I was lucky and fortunate with the timing considering that I had court mandatory anger management classes coming up that week! I had gotten in trouble, non-driving related, and got into a drunken fight in a bar and I got into trouble, so as part of my sentence, I got some probation and some anger management classed.

I was a little doubtful about that the classes at first, considering I am a man, of course, I never really thought that talking about my problems with someone that I didn't know was going to help me, but hey, though I was a bit of a stiff A**hole, I have always been open-minded, so I gave it a try anyway. And considering I had no choice in the matter, what better time than now to be open minded!

I attended a few classes, and in my visits, I not only talked to him about my anger issues, but I also talked about my Road Rage, and you know what, by the third time I had that counselor on the floor dying laughing at a ton of the stories I told him!

I told him a lot about my Road Rage stories, a lot about my heavy drinking, a lot about my anger problems, a lot about me breaking things, and a lot about my crazy home life.

He actually said to me one time, "Wow, you are really are crazy!" in a laughing and funny tone of voice. He could not believe half the things I told him and did, and he did not even know how I was even still alive for the fact of the matter.

If there is one thing I can do good, though, is tell a funny story, even if it is about a bad or crazy situation. I can make just about any story sound funny. We had some great meetings and some good laughs together and I even seen my anger management counselor out at a bar one night like a year later and bought him a drink! It was funny.

While taking the classes, though, what I realized was not that funny. I had some serious control issues, I had some serious anger issues, I had some minor alcohol issues, I had some serious patience problems, and I had some serious Road Rage problems. Not a good combo. I was like a time bomb that was walking and driving around all day long, every day.

I had two meetings a month for about six months at the anger management course. I learned quite a bit from that young man even though he was not much older than I was at the time. I tried to take some of his professional, and friendly, advice that he gave to me from all of our sessions together and I tried to use it in my everyday life.

I had no choice but to grow up a bit after that if I wanted things to change for me. I had to cut back on the drinking or stop altogether. I had to stop getting mad and fighting with people whenever thing did not go my way, whether at home or at work. And I had to stop Road Raging especially!

One thing he told me to also was don't jump to conclusions right away. Just take it easy. Think things out first before you just act. I said in *my* head, "Yeah, sure, that is easy for you to say and do!" But you know what, that whole, think before you act, kind of does work better rather than just acting. Acting out on your first emotion (and for me, that first one was always anger or rage) is the worst one to act out on that will only result in getting you in trouble.

True Story: I am speeding to work one morning because I am late, as usual. As I am speeding down the one-lane road when suddenly someone cuts right out in front of me making me jam on my brakes and nearly causing an accident.

I say right away in my head, "What the F*** is this guy doing?" "Why the hell did he cut me off on purpose like that?!" "Who the hell does he think he is!?" and last I yell out my window at the person, "Come on already, move the F*** out of the way, A** H***!"

I am ready to flip out and snap in two seconds and are not even thinking who might be driving in that car or what is going on.

In the car in front of me is nothing more than a seventy-eight-year-old man who is driving his wife to the supermarket. The man is so old and senile that he cannot even see himself in his rearview mirror with those big black sunglasses on, nor does he know whether he is driving his tank again back in World War II, or if he is driving his 1976 Chevy Impala, so never mind him seeing me driving up behind him doing 90 miles per hour.

So you know I say to myself, "I am late already, who cares if I am five minutes later, at least I won't put other people's lives in danger! And you know what, that old man fought for America in the WWII so that I can drive my car in a free country, and wow, that is amazing that he is still driving at that age, good for him, hope I can do that when I am ninety years old."

It is about being positive rather than negative, being patient, and not blaming others for what is going on all the time, whether it be at home, at work, or on the road.

These are things that we must realize to make the roads safer for everyone instead of doing dangerous and crazy things like Road Raging, cutting people off, and throwing things at them. Patience does take lots of practice and that is the only thing that is going to help you at times when you are stuck behind that old man driving his tank from World War II.

And guess what, from what I realized, the poor old man is already getting yelled at by his wife in the car, and now has me beeping at him for going to slow. Double whammy for the poor old American veteran.

Listen, I know some situations are different, though, and every situation needs to be treated differently. I mean, the guy having a Hummer 3 with rims and the music blasting that just cut you off might have done it on purpose, sure, but this is a real test of your patience. I know you want to get out and bust his tail lights with a baseball bat or follow him to a parking lot and give that son of a B**** a flat tire when he walks into the store, but what good will that do really when you get caught and arrested for doing so? It will only make matters worse for you.

You cannot let anything bother you, especially on the road. You have to learn to let things go, and that is definitely one thing I had a problem with earlier as I told you. I could not let anyone pass me without having to pass them back. It was in my code of honor to never get passed on the road. When I used to get passed on the road I took it as a personal insult, it was like a slap in the face!

Only way I know how to let things go now, I have to pretend that I am "The Great Gandhi" himself at times! I even say some power phrase to myself that he has said like "An eye for an eye makes the world blind" and my anger and Road Rage will subside because "This Too Shall Pass" (I Corinthians 10:12). It is weird but it works.

I also like to use what is called *My Road Rage Buddha*. I have a little bobble head Buddha that I bought at a book store that bounces around on my dashboard. The angrier I get and the faster I drive, the faster he bobbles, and as soon as he does, the sooner he reminds me that I need to slow the F*** down.

It was tough to teach myself to not react on the first universal emotion that I loved so much, RAGE. For some people that is not always there first emotion, but for me it was. That was always my go to feeling. Instead of getting sad, I would get mad and punch a hole in the wall. Instead of getting depressed, I would scream at people. That is all I ever knew and I used to get my way. It is that anger that would turn into RAGE when I was losing my races or when people would cut me off.

But I taught myself how to let go of my anger issues, and how to have some respect for myself, and for others on the road. Before that, I did not have respect for anything. I used to destroy my own vehicles so how could I ever care about anyone else's? That has all changed.

It takes a lot to go from "The Crazy Kid" on the mini bike ripping around town and winning at everything to changing to "The Cool

Adult" that does not get into trouble, and does not yell at people on the road for cutting him off.

But in due time this can be done. It takes a while. For Pete's sake, I was the one who used to Road Rage at people and try to run them off the road for having a peace sign on their car and for being a hippy! "You darn hippies drive too slow and are way too happy!" I would yell at the top of my lungs. Now I am the one with Buddha in my car and driving slow. Who would have ever thought?

Change my friend is a wonderful thing. I am all chilled out now and it is kind of nice. No I am not a pot smoking hippy, but I am laid back, I pray a lot, I have become grateful, and I act respectful and levelheaded. I take my time each day when I drive on the road and you know what; no more tickets, no more cops bust my balls anymore, no more Road Rage altercations, no more smashed cars, no more walking to work, no more high insurance rates, and most importantly, no more time in court. I hate going to court more than anything in life.

So remember, you are talking to the guy that holds the record for getting pulled over more times in one year in his home town than anyone else, twenty-five times, my friends. Like the old saying goes my friend, if I can change, surely you can change.

Hey, you know what Road Rage Buddha says, don't you? ***"Learning how to do things slowly, rather than quickly, in fact, takes no time at all, so slow the hell down and enjoy the ride, buddy!"***

A Poem for the Road

I Like to Speed

I like to speed for many a reason,
I will do it on any day and in any season

Whether the weather be bad, or the weather be fair,
try to pass me on the road if you dare

But I will only warn you once, not twice,
I am faster than a roll of the dice

I love to feel that forceful wind in my face,
when I am passing you on the road in a race

No need for you to try to catch me now,
I am already twenty miles in front you, but how

You could even be that guy driving in his racecar, last name
Schumacher, first name Michael,
but I would even try to pass you if I was on my bicycle

One reason why I like to speed,

is that it gives me that adrenaline fix that I need,

But to get my blood a-flowin',
I got to be doing at least 100 miles per hour to get it going

I am even the kinda guy, whether on two wheels or four,
I will speed the eighth of a mile to the grocery store

I have gotten more speeding tickets,
than the night has crickets

And I have been pulled over more times,
than a rapper has rhymes

And when people say, "One day you will learn your lesson,"
I just reply, "I have escaped death four times already, and I ain't messin'."

I will be speeding until the day I am old and they put me in my wheelchair,
Heck, man, strap a rocket to this thing, too, make it a pair

I am dead now and no longer on the road, no need for worry,
I even told the gravedigger to throw my casket in the ground in a hurry

For speeding is something that I feel as I were born,
Since my first set of wheels, they have been torn

I like to speed for many a reason,

I will do it on any day and in any season

And yes, there is a reason why I do this, indeed,
and that main reason is: I like to speed

- Gennaro Lombardi

CPSIA information can be obtained
at www.ICGtesting.com
Printed in the USA
BVHW051046040123
655554BV00012B/230